CLASSIC
NEW ORLEANS

WILLIAM R. MITCHELL, JR.
PHOTOGRAPHY BY JAMES R. LOCKHART

EDITORIAL ASSISTANCE BY JOHN MAGILL

MARTIN~ST. MARTIN PUBLISHING COMPANY

NEW ORLEANS ◆ SAVANNAH

A GOLDEN COAST BOOK

Dedication

In memory of Thomas B. Holcomb, Jr.,
and F. Monroe Labouisse.

© *1993*
Martin–St. Martin Publishing Company

CLASSIC NEW ORLEANS *and other books by Martin–St. Martin Publishing Company and*
Golden Coast Publishing Company are distributed by
The University of Georgia Press, 330 Research Drive, Athens, GA 30602-4901; telephone (706)369-6130.

Designed and produced by Van Jones Martin,
Golden Coast Publishing Company, Savannah, Georgia.
Cover production and design assistance by Lisa Lytton-Smith, Charlottesville, Virginia.
Edited by John Magill, Van Jones Martin,
Rusty Smith, William R. Mitchell, Jr., and H. Paul St. Martin.
Type set by Golden Coast and Savannah Color Services.
Printed in Hong Kong through Palace Press International, San Francisco, California.

All contemporary color photography © James R. Lockhart.

All archival illustrations were provided by the Historic New Orleans Collection, except as follows:
Louisiana State Museum, 25.1, 28.2, 33.1, 38.1; First Presbyterian Church, 42.2.; Tulane University, xi.1, 50.1;
Xavier University, 53.2; New Orleans Notarial Archives, 67.1, 166.2; Historic American Buildings Survey, National
Park Service, David M. Connick and Susan A. Casente, Spring 1993, 67.3, Tanya Caruso, Fall 1988, 166.3.

The following illustrations are by James Blanchard:
67.4, 106.1, 118.2, 124.1, 125.3, 167.2, 183.1, 219.2, 219.3.

Floor plans were drawn by Frank W. Masson, A.I.A., for Koch and Wilson Architects.
Floor plans were photographed by Jan W. Brantley.

Half-title page: St. Louis Cathedral, Vieux Carré.
Frontispiece: Rodenberg-Gundlach house, Garden District.
Table of contents: Robinson-Jordan house, Garden District.

Library of Congress Catalog Card Number: 93-77933
ISBN 0-8203-1576-1

ACKNOWLEDGMENTS

The New Orleans Architecture Symposium, a collaboration of the Preservation Resource Center of New Orleans, Tulane University, and the Center for Palladian Studies precipitated an interest in a new book on the architecture of New Orleans. This coincided with the plan of the award-winning team of Van Jones Martin and William R. Mitchell to produce a book on our city as part of their series on Southern architecture. We appreciate the contributions of everyone who helped in the creation of *Classic New Orleans*, from its inception to its final form. We particularly want to thank the following people:

Patricia Heatherly Gay, Director, Preservation Resource Center of New Orleans and
Ronald C. Filson, former dean of the Tulane University School of Architecture.
The book coordinators, Jacklyn Jones Derks, Marcelle deBuys Ellis, and H. Paul St. Martin.
The Preservation Resource Center Board, especially Muffin W. Balart, David L. Campbell, Hans A. B. Jonassen,
Frannie Sarpy, Alma Slatten, and Gee Tucker; PRC staff, especially Jan Berry, Jo Bowden, and Sally Cates.
Mario di Valmarana, Edmund Rennolds, and the Center for Palladian Studies.
Museum house personnel, Myrna Bergeron, Curator Pitot House; Harriet P. Bos, Director, Hermann-Grima House;
Patrick Hand, ASID, Curator, 1850 House; Ann Masson, Director, Gallier House;
Alma H. Neal, Director, Beauregard-Keyes House; Dode Platou, Director Emerita and Jon Kukla, Director,
Historic New Orleans Collection; Florence C. Treadway, Director, Longue Vue House and Gardens.
Researchers, Patrice Meese and Kathy Perry.
Tulane University personnel, Wendy Sack and the staff of the School of Architecture;
Joan Caldwell, Louisiana Collection of the Howard Tilton Library;
William Cullison, Southeastern Architectural Archive.
Architects and associates, Franklin Adams, Eugene Cizek, Frank Masson, and Samuel Wilson.
Accommodations for the author, photographer, and his assistant provided by Cary Bond, Eugene Cizek,
Henry Lambert, H. Paul St. Martin, and Lloyd Sensat.
Moral support provided by Jeffrey Pounds, Elizabeth Boggess, Roy Beyer, Cecele Edsberg, John Hoffman, June Jackson,
Nathan Levy, Elizabeth Miles, Ann Seely, Camille Strachan, and Christopher Weeks.
All of the generous homeowners for their enthusiasm and patience and for opening their doors in welcome.

Preservation Resource Center Publications Committee: Henry G. McCall, Chairman
Ann H. Beason, Jane Brooks, David L. Campbell, Jacklyn Jones Derks, Marcelle deBuys Ellis, Ronald C. Filson,
Patricia Heatherly Gay, Julie Hogue McCollam, Michael Myers, H. Paul St. Martin, and Lloyd N. Shields.

Photographing in New Orleans was an experience unlike any I have ever had. Between the rain, the heat, and the marvelous eccentricities of the city, I sometimes wondered if we would ever finish. At the same time, I wanted it to never end. I'll always remember the experiences we had during our time in this unique and exciting city.

The opportunity to participate in the production of this book was given to me by a number of people, each of whom deserves individual acknowledgment. Within that number is a special group without whose support and assistance the work would not have been possible. Among them are my parents, Jack and Charlene Lockhart. Some twenty-odd years ago they gave me a camera, which changed my perceptions, broadened my horizons, and helped me embark on a journey eventually leading to this endeavor.

Acknowledgment also goes to Van Jones Martin, Paul St. Martin, and William R. Mitchell, who entrusted me with the photography for this book. The people of New Orleans deserve special recognition for their hospitality and for allowing us into their homes, as does the Georgia Office of Historic Preservation, for giving me time off from my regular job. Lastly, I want to express my deepest appreciation to my wife, Mary Lee Lockhart, whose assistance and support were invaluable to me in doing this job. To all of you I owe a debt of gratitude and to all of you I want to express my sincere thanks.

James R. Lockhart

TABLE OF CONTENTS

THE PRESERVATION RESOURCE CENTER

The many homes featured in this book are but a sampling of thousands found throughout the City of New Orleans. Over 40,000 buildings are in National Register and local historic districts, a result of the fact that New Orleans grew to be such a large city in the early nineteenth century (having become the fourth city in the United States to reach a population of 100,000) and because New Orleans citizens have been so successful in historic preservation efforts.

Since its founding in 1974, the Preservation Resource Center of New Orleans has been supported by generous gifts from the community. Initially funded by a grant from the Junior League of New Orleans, the PRC has more than 4,000 members and an annual fundraising program that together make possible special projects and ongoing services in historic preservation. With a charge to promote the preservation of historic architecture and neighborhoods citywide, the PRC has always regarded preservation of the historic built environment as a means to enhance and preserve the livability of the City of New Orleans.

The PRC presents statements from three major supporters and lists donors as evidence of a strong preservation ethic in New Orleans and belief in the city's unique heritage as a major factor in the quality of life of all citizens. We thank the following donors and join with them to celebrate the publication of *Classic New Orleans* and its role in promoting the historic architecture and neighborhoods of New Orleans.

Patricia H. Gay
Preservation Resource Center

City of New Orleans

Unlike many large cities in the United States, New Orleans is noted throughout the world for its unique architectural style and distinctive spirit. Perhaps it is our extraordinary history, which boasts a fine mixture of ethnic influences, such as French, Indian, African, Spanish, Irish, and German; or perhaps it is the way our community has managed to create an environment which blends old-world charm with new-world vitality. Whatever the origin, New Orleans is a city boasting a large inventory of historic and architecturally dramatic structures like no other city.

The historic neighborhoods of New Orleans contribute significantly to the development and vitality of our community. Residents and visitors alike appreciate and value this asset. *Classic New Orleans* can play an important part in preserving and promoting this important element of our city.

Classic New Orleans brings together carefully researched and composed articles and visually exquisite photographs, producing a valuable and educational publication which enables the rest of the world to view our style as well. I congratulate the Preservation Resource Center and the Tulane School of Architecture for their help in this project.

Mayor Sidney Barthelemy, City of New Orleans, 1993

Bisso Towboat Company

We must remember that New Orleans is a great port city, and its history, commerce, and culture are inextricably linked to the Mississippi. Our family has been a part of that history, operating the same towboat company for five generations. When steam-powered vessels began replacing sailing ships, we were there, supplying them with coal. In fact, our oldest tug was honored by the PRC in 1990 for an amazing 105 years on the river.

Our family has a rich maritime heritage in New Orleans and is committed to the preservation of the historic integrity of our port city. Bisso salutes the publication of *Classic New Orleans* and supports the positive role the Preservation Resource Center plays in our community. We're part of the history and growth of New Orleans and believe in the importance of maintaining our city's historic neighborhoods and architecture for future generations.

William A. Slatten, Bisso Towboat Company, 1993

Freeport McMoRan, Inc.

The heart of New Orleans is its historic neighborhoods, and this firm belief is what guides our company as it directs much of its philanthropic funidng to neighborhood rejuvenation. When Freeport McMoRan moved its corporate headquarters from New York City to New Orleans in 1985, one of its first community investments in its expanded charitable giving program was a donation to the Preservation Resource Center. Since that time the company's gifts to the PRC have more than quadrupled and its commitment to neighborhood revitalization has strengthened many times over.

Jim Bob Moffett, Chairman, Chief Executive Officer, and President of Freeport McMoRan, Inc., 1993

Preservation Resource Center, 604 Julia Street

The Preservation Resource Center is grateful to the following donors who commend the publication of *Classic New Orleans* and support the "Living In New Orleans Campaign," which promotes home ownership in the historic neighborhoods of New Orleans.

Joe W. and Dorothy Dorsett Brown Foundation   ~   Joseph C. and Sue Ellen M. Canizaro Foundation
Mr. and Mrs. Arthur Q. Davis   ~   Graham Resources   ~   Latter & Blum
Mr. and Mrs. J. Thomas Lewis   ~   Magnolia Marketing Company   ~   Waldemar Nelson & Company, Inc.
Levy-Rosenblum Foundation
Mr. and Mrs. Hirschel T. Abbott, Jr.   ~   Dr. and Mrs. Kenneth N. Adatto   ~   Lucile and Gerald Andrus
Dr. and Mrs. Luis A. Balart   ~   Amos T. Beason   ~   Blumenthal Print Works, Inc.
David L. Campbell   ~   Mr. and Mrs. William K. Christovich   ~   Mrs. Kyser Cox   ~   Mr. and Mrs. Gerald A. Derks
Mr. and Mrs. D. Blair Favrot   ~   Mr. and Mrs Wyn Howard
Mr. and Mrs. Lawrence Israel   ~   Mr. Lester E. Kabacoff   ~   Mr. Tom Jeffris
Mrs. James M. Lapeyre   ~   Mr. and Mrs. Henry George McCall II   ~   Mr. and Mrs. John M. McCollam
Martha W. Murphy   ~   Mr. and Mrs. Paul S. Murphy   ~   Mr. and Mrs. Robert J. Newman
Dr. and Mrs. Lincoln Denton Paine   ~   Barbara and Winston Rice   ~   Mr. and Mrs. Michael X. St. Martin
Mr. and Mrs. R. Henry Sarpy, Jr.   ~   Mr. James Stone   ~   Mrs. Frank G. Strachan
Dr. and Mrs. Richard L. Strub   ~   Mr. and Mrs. George G. Villere   ~   Ben Weiner
Judge and Mrs. David R. M. Williams   ~   Tina Freeman and Philip Woollam

The following Major Donors—many from Operation Comeback's and Christmas in October's
earliest days—also deserve recognition.

Alerion Bank; Mr. and Mrs. Jack Aron; Azby Fund; Estate of Armande Billion; Boh Foundation; Booth-Bricker Fund; CNG Producing Company; Chevron U.S.A. Inc.; Continental Underwriters, Ltd.; Copeland's; Cox Cable of New Orleans, Inc.; Deloitte & Touche; Delta Queen Steamboat Company; Deutsch, Kerrigan, & Stiles; Collins C. Diboll Foundation; Downmann Family Foundation; Mrs. William B. Dreux (deceased); Entergy/LP&L/NOPSI; Exxon U.S.A.; Thomas Favrot; Federal National Mortgage Association Foundation; Fidelity Homestead Association; First National Bank of Commerce; Gheens Foundation; The Greater New Orleans Foundation; Mr. and Mrs. G. G. Griswold II; Helis Foundation; Mrs. Jimmy Heymann; Hibernia National Bank; The Home Depot; IBM Corporation; IDS/American Express; Eugenie and Joseph Jones Family Foundation; Junior League of New Orleans; Keller Family Foundation; J. B. Levert Foundation; Louisiana Land & Exploration; McDermott International, Inc.; Mobil Exploration & Producing U.S., Inc.; J. Edgar Monroe Foundation; Dr. David A. Newsome; Pan American Life Insurance Company; Parkside Foundation; Premier Bank; Proctor & Gamble; The Reily Foundation; Rice, Fowler, Kingsmill, Vance, Flint, & Booth; Mrs. Francoise B. Richardson; RosaMary Foundation; Secor Bank; Shell Oil Company Foundation; Simon, Peragine, Smith, & Redfearn; Southern Baptist Hospital; State of Louisiana; Texaco, U.S.A.; Touro Infirmary; Union Pacific Foundation (U. P. Realty); Ambassador and Mrs. John G. Weinmann; Whitney National Bank; Councilman Peggy Wilson, City Council NOPSI Fund; Mary Freeman Wisdom Foundation; WJS Copy Machine

THE HISTORIC NEW ORLEANS COLLECTION
529–33 Royal Street

In the New Orleans *Item* of May 5, 1938, Harnett T. Kane wrote, "The most important exchange of property since the renaissance of interest began in the city's Vieux Carré a few years ago was revealed . . . in a real estate and restoration project of nationwide importance."

Kane's article referred to the purchase by General and Mrs. L. Kemper Williams of what was then called the Casa Grande, or Miro House. Mistakenly thought to have been the home of Governor Don Esteban Miro, it is now called the Merieult House in honor of its builder, Jean François Merieult.

Originally purchased by General and Mrs. Williams to serve as their home, the Merieult House, along with several other buildings, now house the Historic New Orleans Collection, a renowned museum and research center for state and local history and the source for almost all of the archival images used in *Classic New Orleans*. These structures are among the most important, historically and architecturally, in the Vieux Carré. Containing libraries and archives, a museum, the Williamses' residence, and a rare and important collection of Louisiana material, the Historic New Orleans Collection is still growing and is open to the public.

Jean François Merieult, a successful international merchant-trader, began building his Royal Street house in 1792 over rubble from an earlier structure leveled by the great fire of 1788. The Merieult House today contains a series of galleries, a library, and a gift shop. When it was built, the ground floor housed the offices and storerooms of Merieult's thriving import business, as well as several rented stores. The second floor served as the family's living quarters. The house survived the city's second great fire in 1794 and stands as one of the oldest structures in New Orleans, although in a somewhat altered state.

The façade of the original building, which was of stuccoed brick, consisted of a series of rounded arches along the ground floor, while along the second floor there were French doors and a wooden balcony over which the tile roof extended.

In 1795 and 1796 Merieult built warehouses for his import business adjoining the original building and surrounding the formal courtyard behind his home. In 1798 he bought the key lot on the back of the property fronting Toulouse Street and built stables and another warehouse.

Following Merieult's death in 1818, the property went through a succession of owners. In 1832 the international banking firm of Lizardi Brothers purchased the house and compound and made extensive alterations. The granite-columned façade of the original house took on much of its present appearance at that time.

The Lizardis renovated the 1795 warehouse and added a second floor. The first floor was converted to a large Greek Revival style counting house. Today the Counting House is the main meeting and reception room of the Historic New Orleans Collection. The upstairs of this building and the renovated 1796 warehouse now serve as museum offices.

In 1878 Jean Baptiste Trapolin bought the property, converted the three front buildings into a small hotel, and demolished the stable and 1798 warehouse. On the site of the stable-warehouse, he built his family residence in 1889. When General and Mrs. Williams purchased the property in 1938, they initiated a major renovation and restoration project for the entire compound, retaining the Trapolin home as the main rooms of their residence and creating apartments and guest rooms in the other buildings. In 1944 the Williamses purchased the early nineteenth-century building at 720–24 Toulouse Street and converted it into a garage and chauffeur's quarters. It was restored to its original appearance in 1976 and now houses the manuscripts division of the collection. Playwright Tennessee Williams rented an attic apartment here for several months in 1938–39.

A c. 1840 townhouse on Toulouse Street currently houses museum offices and the Richard Koch Reading Room. A small cottage nearby was purchased and will be used for offices, and in March 1993 the Historic New Orleans Collection purchased the 1915 Police and Court Building at 410 Chartres Street, which will be renovated to support the continued growth of this remarkable collection in the heart of the Vieux Carré.

The main courtyard of the Historic New Orleans Collection, painted by Boyd Cruise in 1950.

TULANE UNIVERSITY

Richardson Memorial Building; School of Architecture, Tulane University.

The Tulane School of Architecture is pleased to support this book on the architecture of New Orleans. The grand homes illustrated herein are indeed a "classic" portion of the architecture that makes New Orleans such a fascinating city. These residences begin to reveal the variety of design influences and cultural values—European, African, Caribbean, and even, in the twentieth century, International—that have contributed richness and vitality to the city's physical setting.

Constituted as a "fabric city" favoring a neighborhood's *tout ensemble* over any one artifact, New Orleans possesses an architecture intriguing and seductive. This fabric of buildings interweaves with a teeming natural landscape of courtyard, parkland, river, lake, and swamp; commingled, these forms define the city's physical and historic values. Most of the structures shown date from the nineteenth century, as of course does much of New Orleans. However, this book's valuable Timeline brings us through the twentieth century, an era also important to include in the history of New Orleans, if we are to give her full credit.

Beginning with the first architecture courses taught in 1894, the Tulane faculty has involved itself with both preservation of our historic environment and design of significant new forms. We instill in our students a sensitivity for our cityscape, teaching enhancement of the old while introducing the new; the city serves as our learning laboratory, in all parts of its cultural and historical makeup. We are expanding our programs in historic preservation and environmental conservation, towards a full professionalism that addresses both that for which we are nostalgic, and that which challenges our inevitably preconceived opinions about architectural, historical, or cultural significance. In this way we can help preservation efforts in New Orleans meet the challenges of contemporary and future urban needs.

Donna V. Robertson,
Dean of the Architecture School
Tulane University, 1993

FOREWORD

CLASSIC NEW ORLEANS is the third in a series of books on the architectural history of Southern cities. Bill Mitchell and I collaborated on *Classic Savannah* (1987) and *Classic Atlanta* (1991) as author and photographer and co-editors with the confidence of natives—I was born in Savannah and Bill in Atlanta. Creating a book on New Orleans, as we were to discover, was a different kettle of crawfish. It was a challenging, invigorating, and completely fascinating experience.

As a child, long before I dreamed of working on such a series, New Orleans was just the place where Georgia Tech played in the Sugar Bowl several times in the 1950s. Newspaper photographs of my heroes posing in the French Quarter and black-and-white television images of the bowl parades gently poked my curiosity. Years later, but before I ever ventured farther west than Valdosta, Georgia, books, newspapers, television, and movies had smuggled a variety of superficial but vivid impressions into my head—from

Mardi Gras merrymakers in front of the Henry Clay Monument on Canal Street in 1893, from Frank Leslie's Illustrated Newpaper.

Yancey Derringer and *Bourbon Street Beat* to *All the King's Men* and Clarence John Laughlin. I pictured New Orleans as an odd combination of Philadelphia, Natchez, and Daytona Beach.

Today, after many visits to the Crescent City, I know why New Orleans is a name so exotically evocative it conjures up a flow of images and sensations like no other place in the United States: Mardi Gras, Cajuns, Creoles, cast-iron balconies, French doors, and the mighty Mississippi; swamps, bayous, alligators, crawfish, floods, hurricanes, and above-ground cemeteries; gumbo, blues, Dixie beer, Hurricanes, and brass band funerals; Al Hirt, Pete Fountain, Preservation Hall, the Neville Brothers, the Marsalis family, Clifton Chenier, and the *Ballad of New Orleans*; Andy Jackson, La Salle, Jean Lafitte, P. G. T. Beauregard, and Huey Long; William Faulkner, Tennessee Williams, and Anne Rice; *The Big Easy* and *Easy*

Rider; James Gallier and Jim Garrison; *A Streetcar Named Desire* and *A Confederacy of Dunces*; Tulane, Newcomb, Dillard, UNO, and Loyola; Bourbon Street, St. Charles Avenue, Elysian Fields, and Esplanade; Bayou St. John and Lake Pontchartrain; beignets and Community Coffee; Storyville, Algiers, and the Garden District; strippers and cover charges; Latrobe and Latrobe; mosquitoes and yellow fever; Dakin and Dakin; the St. Charles Hotel and the Superdome; Jackson Square and Audubon Park; Greek Revival mansions and shotgun cottages; steamboats and streetcars; red beans and rice; jazz and Spanish moss; heat and humidity.

Native New Orleanians, historically from Indian, Spanish, French, African, English, Irish, Italian, and German origins and a multitude of combinations thereof, naturally express a relaxed familiarity with the customs, pace, directions, and pronunciations peculiar to their city. And while casual tourists and conventioneers stumble briefly over names like *Vieux Carré*, they generally see the city as an easygoing, sexy, free-spirited old town of parties, antiques, and souvenirs. For the truly inquisitive, however, New Orleans can be an almost overwhelming experience of wild beauty and sad decay, innate complexity and studied contradictions.

Therefore, producing a book about "classic" New Orleans presented immediate and considerable problems. The confluence of cultures has formed combinations of languages and styles that are seductive and unique, yet sometimes exasperating. When stirred by the passage of time, the history of New Orleans is further muddied—confusing even the most diligent scholar or lifelong native.

As the first European explorers traveled down the Mississippi, the current carried them through the delta to the Gulf of Mexico. The current was their engine and their guide. From the Gulf, however, going back to find the mouth of the great river among the thousands of channels, bays, and islands literally took years. Studying the history of New Orleans and its architecture is like sailing in the Gulf, searching for the Mississippi as it spreads amid its alluvial islands—the subtle and confusing changes of time make defining it a matter of perspective, persistence, and local knowledge.

Early in the project I learned that even something so basic to the study of a place as its geography presents an additional challenge in New Orleans. The Mississippi River flows from north to south, and New Orleans is on the east bank, simple enough. But when the river gets to southern Louisiana it makes a long, gentle turn to the east, so New Orleans is actually due *north* of it, on the *east* bank, which, in the nineteenth century, many locals referred to as the *left* bank. As if the essential terminology were not baffling enough, man and nature have conspired throughout the history of the city to physically alter the landscape—the river flooding and eroding, the population damming and draining. The Mississippi is erratic, but inexorable, and, as we will see, it has been the single most important factor in shaping the character of its Crescent City.

From the beginning, the port city has been more a bouillabaisse than a melting pot, its many disparate components retaining very distinct characteristics while still contributing to the overall flavor. After all, it was established by a company owned by a Scot under the flag of France, and later had a Spanish governor named O'Reilly. It is no wonder then, as the territory and city have passed through time from one cultural influence to another, the names of streets, faubourgs (New Orleans suburbs), and landmarks were changed accordingly. For example, the Bienville Plantation was subdivided by the Gravier family and thus called Ville Gravier; it was subsequently named Faubourg Ste. Marie, anglicized somewhat to Faubourg St. Mary, generalized to the American Sector, and is now referred to as the Central Business District!

It should also not be surprising that a population surrounded by a fluid environment and descended through a multicultural history should be so flexible when defining itself. "Creole" is a term familiar to all New Orleanians, but its definition is imprecise at best, differing sometimes from citizen to citizen, neighborhood to neighborhood. Similarly, the designations and boundaries for faubourgs, neighborhoods, and historic districts sometimes seem to be a matter of taste, timing, or personal inclination. His-

toric district boundaries often depend on whether one is discussing local, state, or national designation. To avoid confusing either visitors or natives, we have tried to give clear descriptions of neighborhoods and use consistent terminology throughout the book.

Our methodology and objectives in creating *Classic New Orleans* are similar to those Bill and I pursued in *Classic Savannah* and *Classic Atlanta*: to reflect on the history of the city; describe its neighborhoods and architectural evolution using archival images and contemporaneous quotes; and illustrate landmark examples of its residential architecture—presenting them all in a provocative and beautiful package in a sincere effort to portray the essence of New Orleans and proclaim the paramount importance of its preservation. To underscore that point we are proud to recognize the invaluable assistance of many tireless heroes of the New Orleans preservation movement, most notably the Preservation Resource Center, the Tulane University School of Architecture, and the Historic New Orleans Collection. The PRC, led by the enthusiasm of Patty Gay, contributed many hours helping Bill and Paul St. Martin choose the featured homes. John Magill of the Historic New Orleans Collection selected almost all of the archival illustrations and checked the manuscript for accuracy.

Our large production team consisted of writers, photographers, editors, and historians—all preservationists, each painfully aware of the erosion and loss of our physical and cultural heritage. The archival illustrations in the timeline and gazetteer may often be melancholy reminders of lost treasures, but Jim Lockhart's striking contemporary photographs of landmark homes are beacons of hope. Like two-way mirrors in which we see reflections of our past and views of the future, these wonderful old houses are living homes to a proud, vital population ready to enter the twenty-first century. There are fascinating museum houses and inspiring examples of meticulously restored private homes, but more often we recognize how modern families preserve by adapting—fitting the demands of contemporary life within the charming and distinctive context of earlier eras. We congratulate those who have fought so hard to preserve the best characteristics fundamental to this unique American city. We hope that others may find within these pages the inspiration to join this noble effort.

Van Jones Martin
February 8, 1993

PREFACE

"Across the second story a grillwork balcony, so deliciously wrought that it looked like iron lace. . . ."
Frances Cavanah, *Louis of New Orleans*

I GREW UP ON THE LOVELY STEREOTYPES of the travel writing and pictures in *Holiday* magazine, and visions of sugar plums for me were pralines from the French Quarter. The words *Vieux Carré* were not yet in my vocabulary in 1947 when my parents went to an insurance convention in New Orleans. They left me at home in Atlanta with an aunt and my older sister (who did not feel left behind at all). I was nine, and I envied my parents. They came back with a souvenir booklet from Antoine's; I still remember reading about Creole cooking, Oysters Rockefeller, and private dining rooms as old as Atlanta.

My parents drank Sazeracs, I recall, and wine flowed in ways it didn't in Atlanta. I can still imagine the way I thought coffee and beignets must have tasted at the French Market. I heard about Tujague's and naughty Bourbon Street and antique shops on famous Royal Street. They brought me picture postcards with multistory, cast-iron balconies turning corners where people watched Mardi Gras parades.

My admiration for the place my parents had been was unbounded. In my mind's eye it had become far better than *Holiday* magazine's color photographs had tantalizingly touted it. In fact, in my grammar school mind, I became a tout—maybe I still am—for the eccentric magic this old and complex American city has come to represent. It seemed like an obtainable Paris. One didn't even have to cross the Mississippi. It was as though one might be able to walk there, right across Lake Pontchartrain. As a young adult, I finally made it to the Vieux Carré and the Garden District. I stayed at The Royal Orleans and, if anything,

the tourist's experience was better than I had imagined.

In 1986 the opportunity to write a book about New Orleans began to materialize; I had just completed the text for a book on Savannah architecture and was attending a meeting in Charleston where I met for the first time Paul St. Martin, a fellow preservationist who lives in the Crescent City. The next year, on a trip to New Orleans, I presented Paul a newly published copy of *Classic Savannah*, and we resumed our discussions about a similar book on New Orleans. I soon spoke with Van Jones Martin, my long-time collaborator and the owner of Golden Coast Publishing Company, regarding the possible project. Eventually, during the time Van and I were working on *Classic Atlanta*, we all met in New Orleans with interested representatives of the Tulane School of Architecture and the Preservation Resource Center and began serious planning. By the fall of 1990, Paul and Van had established a new publishing company, Martin-St. Martin, and the lengthy process of producing *Classic New Orleans* was finally begun.

The Cabildo and Jackson Square by William Woodward, 1905

It was a dream come true, even at my age, to do a book about New Orleans, "classic" New Orleans—to dwell, for a time, on it and in it, not just visit for a long weekend. My New Orleans research headquarters for a part of 1991 was an upstairs guest suite in the ell at Paul St. Martin's restored 1850s home in the Lower Garden District. From that intimate vantage, or back at home in Atlanta, where I did most of the writing, I wondered: "Are classic and cliché, in this context, synonymous? Have I seen beyond the oversimplified, uncritical judgement of a place of childhood dreams and given the city and its buildings palpable reality, mature and adult significance?"

There is, of course, a fine line between classic and cliché, between true essence and superficial assumptions.

Over time and with succeeding generations a place evolves, and some periods and parts of the evolution are more beautiful and interesting than others. Some aspects persist and become symbolic; something "in the blood," a spirit, prevails. Sometimes, in fact, clear traditions have been formed, landmarks built and preserved in the flux of time, which are widely known and respected. This is what our book addresses: classic New Orleans as embodied in architecture and buildings; parks, gardens, trees, squares, and streets—the physical setting; houses and neighborhoods, many, many of which are officially designated historic districts. Our book is about where and how its citizens live, today, in what they have inherited from this evolution.

What and where is this classic New Orleans? Is it all pervasive throughout the city? What about the place is clearly *there*? Gertrude Stein said about a California suburb, "There is no there, there." Such has never been said about New Orleans. It is a there, that is clearly, firmly, and characteristically there. A there that is made up of many parts which have evolved together in time and space. This is what our book is about.

A classic view from a French Quarter balcony, 1992.

What assertions are most easily made that are simply true about the place once called La Nouvelle-Orléans? What accretions are clear demarcations? How did it become the way it is? What characteristics can we identify? And, in addressing the *tout ensemble* of the entire parish-wide city—not just of the Vieux Carré–can we help to assure its continued persistence? What is the style of the place now, as a result of its evolution out of a diverse past? Is there a unity out of its many sectors, neighborhoods, and districts? Where are the aspects in the large metropolis spreading out from the Mississippi to Bayou St. John to Lake Pontchartrain that most give it life and meaning?

What are the schoolhouse simplicities, the classic simplicities, one should know? What is the recipe for New Orleans? Are the ingredients as Creole as one has always been told? In *A Streetcar Named Desire*, Tennessee Williams has a character say: "New Orleans isn't like other cities." That it is not "like other cities" seems to be canonical, an article of faith, its very constitution, written and unwritten.

I expect the New Orleans of my childhood, the New Orleans of *Holiday*, *National Geographic*, *Life*, and the newsreels—my beloved cliché—is the New Orleans all of us want to experience, but it is a real place I have tried to present with the help of many concerned people. We have all conspired together to present a grownup's dream of the Crescent City, a place we want to see preserved so that future generations may also know it as we have.

We ask ourselves, of course, will the love of the place by people like ourselves who believe in it and cherish it, assure its continued life with all of its eccentric magic intact? We do not want future generations to only read about it in this and other books; we do not want it to become a Clarence John Laughlin ghost, a mirage, a carnival charade, God forbid, a pretty nightmare masquerading as a possible dream. We want future generations to be able to do their own books on classic New Orleans, a place of recognized value, a standard of excellence, authentic and enduring.

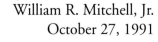

William R. Mitchell, Jr.
October 27, 1991

INTRODUCTION:
From Orléans to La Nouvelle-Orléans to New Orleans

La Salle claiming Louisiana for France.

ORLÉANS, FRANCE, seventy-five miles southwest of Paris on the river Loire, evolved from the Roman city, Aurelianum, which had been built on the site of an ancient Gallic town Julius Caesar destroyed in 52 B.C. From the Latin name, Aurelianum (probably named for Marcus Aurelius), the French derived Orléans. Almost three centuries after Joan of Arc was immortalized as the Maid of Orléans for raising the English siege there in 1428, France established La Nouvelle-Orléans in the French colony of La Louisiane, a New World away on the Mississippi River.

From settlements in the upper Mississippi Valley, France had sent explorers downriver in the latter part of the seventeenth century seeking the mouth of the great river and a strategic advantage in the New World competition with Spain and England. In 1682, an expedition led by René-Robert Cavelier, Sieur de La Salle, reached the Gulf of Mexico and claimed for France the entire territory through which they had traveled, naming it La Louisiane, for Louis XIV.

Locating the mouth of the Mississippi when approaching from the Gulf proved even more difficult, however. La Salle failed in an attempt on a return trip with settlers in 1684, and fifteen years passed before French-Canadian Pierre Le Moyne, Sieur d'Iberville, sailing west along the Gulf Coast from a French settlement at Mobile Bay, finally rediscovered it in 1699.

Seeking to blunt Spanish expansion from Florida, France tried to establish outposts in the area with little success for another eighteen years before finally, in 1717, the management of the entire territory was turned over to an entrepreneur, Scottish financial genius John Law, and his holding company, known at the time as the Compagnie d'Occident (Company of the West) and later as the

Company of the Indies and the Mississippi Company. A strategic settlement near the mouth of the river was to be an integral part of Law's ambitious plan. In 1718, Iberville's brother, Jean-Baptiste Le Moyne, Sieur de Bienville, selected a town site about 100 miles upstream from the stormy Gulf at the Indian portage to Bayou St. John and Lake Pontchartrain. The name, La Nouvelle-Orléans, honored Louis Philippe Joseph (1674-1723), duc d'Orléans, the colorful but insolvent Prince Regent of France, who had aided Law in a European banking scheme.

By 1719 European speculation in shares of Law's company had caused its value to soar, but inflation began to threaten his paper empire, and in 1720 panic selling brought him to ruin. Law's "Mississippi Bubble" had burst, but in Louisiana Bienville persevered. In 1720 military engineer Pierre Le Blond de la Tour designed a town plan while at Biloxi, and in 1721 his assistant, Adrien de Pauger, took it to La Nouvelle-Orléans and began laying out the streets. The original plan consisted of a grid of streets around a central parade ground, the Place d'Armes, and it is still evident in the Vieux Carré (literally, Old Square, also popularly known as the French Quarter). A census in 1721 showed a population of 470, including 277 whites, 172 black slaves, and 21 Indian slaves. This was a rough frontier settlement, with rude housing offering little comfort from an inhospitable environment. The earliest settlers were French-Canadians, Swiss, and Germans.

In 1722 La Nouvelle-Orléans was made the capital of La Louisiane, and the colony remained French until 1762. According to the treaty ending the French and Indian War, France agreed to cede to England its Canadian territories and claims to lands east of the Mississippi, except for the Isle of Orleans. (The area immediately around New Orleans is virtually an island surrounded by

ABOVE: Louisiana Purchase transfer ceremonies in the Place d'Armes.
BELOW: The Battle of New Orleans.

swamps and bayous, the Mississippi, and Lake Pontchartrain.) At the same time France arranged a secret agreement promising the Isle of Orleans and the Louisiana Territory west of the Mississippi to the Spanish. In 1768 when Spain actually began governing the city, a small rebellion revealed that the spirited soul of the place would not be easily tamed nor gladly lose its Gallic ways. After two disastrous fires (1788 and 1794), the city was almost totally rebuilt during Spanish rule, and, although some street names and building styles reflect the Spanish influence, the city retained much of its French character.

Under another secret arrangement in 1800, Spain returned control of the territory to France, and in 1803 Napoleon approved the sale of the colony to the youthful United States during the presidency of Thomas Jefferson. The population of New Orleans at the time of the Louisiana Purchase was approximately 8,000: 4,000 whites, 2,700 black slaves, and about 1,300 "free persons of color." The population ballooned the following year when 5,797 refugees of the Santo Domingo slave uprising arrived. Among them were almost 2,000 free persons of color who spoke French and were generally well-educated or had trades. Ultimately, almost 10,000 Santo Domingan refugees came to New Orleans, significantly influencing the character of the city from that time forward.

Many of the new immigrants referred to themselves as Creole, meaning they were of European descent and born in the French or Spanish colonies. Over time a variance of the word in New Orleans evolved to also mean any local mixture of Spanish, French, African, or American ancestry. While to many people this may be at odds with the original definition, it is a usage with deep roots in Crescent City history.

The city first expanded upriver from the Vieux Carré, along the natural levee into the Faubourg Ste. Marie (St.

Introduction

Mary), which was laid out in 1788 and became the "American Sector." In 1806, one year after the city incorporated, Faubourg Marigny was established downriver and adjacent to the Vieux Carré. The pattern of American settlement upriver and French and Creole settlement in the Vieux Carré and downriver generally continued as other faubourgs (suburbs) were eventually subdivided from the large plantations surrounding the original town.

In 1812 Louisiana became the eighteenth state to join the Union. That year, formal hostilities resumed with

New Orleans, 1852.

England, and three years later, in the last battle of the War of 1812 (actually fought after a treaty had been signed but not ratified), Andrew Jackson led a ragtag force that rescued the city from the invading British army. The citizens of New Orleans turned out for a gala celebration for Jackson in the Place d'Armes, which in 1851 was renamed Jackson Square in his honor.

As the Mississippi Valley became more densely settled and trade expanded, the port of New Orleans grew dramatically. Steamboats made freight traffic on the strong

river more feasible and immensely profitable. The cotton trade alone was having an extraordinary influence, and by 1840 New Orleans was, by some measures, the fourth busiest port in the world and home to more than 100,000 people, making it the largest city in the South and the fourth largest in the nation. To the French, Spanish, African, Creole, and Anglo-American population came large numbers of immigrants from Ireland and Germany. The spectacular growth of these decades is given sad perspective by the effects of the 1853 yellow fever epidemic. Eight thousand people died, a staggering toll equal to the total population of the city when the territory was transferred only fifty years before. Despite the health and sanitary problems that accompanied its geography and climate, by the beginning of the Civil War New Orleans had become a cosmopolitan gem of fascinating culture and sophisticated architecture.

As it would throughout the South, the war stunted the growth of New Orleans, but competition from rail-

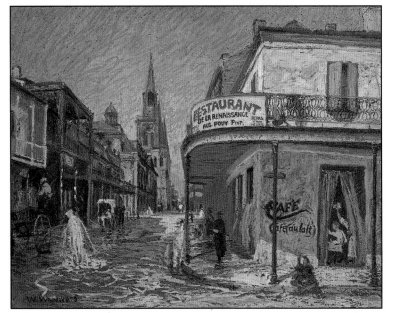

TOP: Canal Street at St. Charles, 1900. ABOVE: Vieux Carré, c. 1904.
OPPOSITE: St. Louis Cathedral and Jackson Square, 1992.

roads and northern canals had already begun to diminish the traffic through the port. Captured by Union forces sailing up the Mississippi in 1862, the city remained under military command for the remainder of the war, and the Louisiana state government operated under the reorganization laws of Reconstruction until 1877. The boom times never quite returned to their antebellum heights, but the city continued to prosper for the rest of the century.

As its population grew, the Crescent City spread beyond both banks of the river. Many of the early faubourgs were absorbed into the city, and by 1874, the boundaries of the City of New Orleans had grown to their current configuration, encompassing 199 square miles. The extensive swamps that stretched away from the old city toward the lake were drained and filled, and the incorporation of a mechanical drainage system in the early 1900s permitted their development. Some of contemporary New Orleans is actually as much as five feet below sea level—kept relatively dry during rainy seasons by

this massive drainage network and its ingenious pumping stations.

Much of the character we associate with New Orleans was shaped prior to World War I. The advances in transportation, communications, and technology since that time have had a gross homogenizing effect on American cities, so that modern downtown New Orleans has a tendency to look more and more like similar areas in Birmingham or Louisville or even Tampa. Fortunately, the bland impression of sameness one might get from a distant perspective of the New Orleans skyline is misleading, for once within the city, whether strolling the sidewalks of the Vieux Carré or riding a streetcar along St. Charles Avenue, one is surely in the Crescent City. The enduring charms of her multifarious cultures have combined to create the "classic" New Orleans we seek—especially in the architecture, decorative arts, and gardens—and these cultures continue to be lived and enlivened, to evolve, and be interpreted even until the present day. It is, after all, this mélange, this gumbo, this jazz, as it were, which characterizes this place first called La Nouvelle-Orléans.

NEW ORLEANS TIMELINE

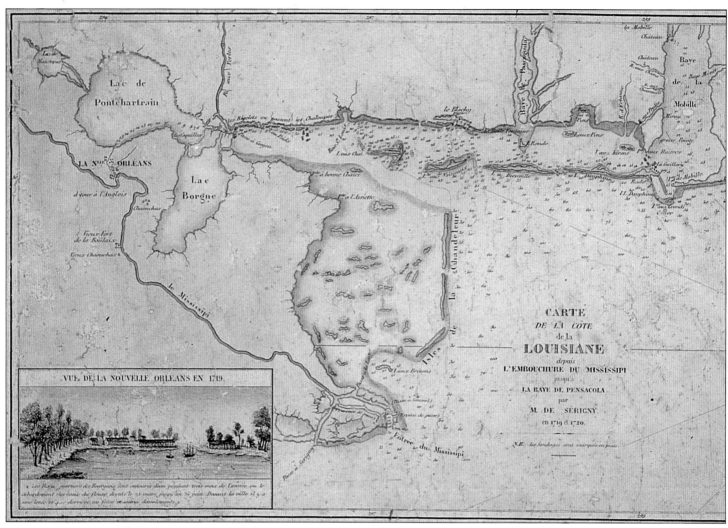

VUE DE LA NOUVELLE ORLÉANS EN 1719

CARTE
DE LA CÔTE
de la
LOUISIANE
depuis
L'EMBOUCHURE DU MISSISSIPI
jusqu'à
LA BAYE DE PENSACOLA
par
M. DE SÉRIGNY
en 1719 à 1720.

The Louisiana coast and the area around La Nouvelle-Orléans, by de Serigny, 1719–20. [22.1]

1682   April 9. René-Robert Cavelier, Sieur de La Salle (1648–1687), claimed Louisiana territory in the name of Louis XIV.

1699   Pierre Le Moyne, Sieur d'Iberville (1661–1706), explored the entrance to the Mississippi River, naming the mouth Pointe du Mardi Gras. The expedition also named Lake Pontchartrain and Bayou St. John.

1712   Antoine Crozat (1655–1738), a wealthy French merchant, was granted trading rights in Louisiana.

1717   Crozat relinquished his trade concession to John Law's Company of the West, which was instrumental in colonizing Louisiana.

1718   French-Canadian Jean-Baptiste Le Moyne, Sieur de Bienville (1680–1768), established La Nouvelle-Orléans and named it in honor of Louis Philippe Joseph, duc d'Orléans, Prince Regent of France.

We are working at Nouvelle Orléans with as much zeal as the shortage of men will permit. I have myself conveyed over the spot to select a place where it will be best to locate the settlement. All the ground of the site, except the borders, which are drowned by floods, is very good, and everything will grow there.
Jean-Baptiste Le Moyne, Sieur de Bienville
Diary, June 1718

1720   Population of Louisiana: 6,000.

First black slaves brought to Louisiana.

John Law's "Mississippi Bubble" collapsed.

1721 Gridiron town plan drawn by Pierre Le Blond de la Tour (d. 1723) and laid out by Adrien de Pauger (d. 1726). Streets named for saints and for French royalty and nobility.

1722 New Orleans named capital of the Louisiana colony; Bienville was governor until his recall to France in 1725.

Barracks erected along Toulouse Street, designed by de la Tour and de Pauger.

1724 *Code Noir* promulgated for regulation of black slaves in Louisiana.

Claude Dubreuil built first man-made levee at New Orleans.

Director's house erected near the corner of Decatur and Toulouse streets, designed by de la Tour and de Pauger. [23.1]

Director's house, drawn by Henry W. Krotzer from plans in the French National Archive. (23.1)

New Orleans is growing before our eyes, and there is no longer any doubt that it is going to become a great city.
Adrien de Pauger, January 1724

Roman Catholicism became state religion.

Parish Church of St. Louis begun; designed by de la Tour and de Pauger, completed in 1727. [23.2]

Parish Church of St. Louis, in the Place d'Armes, by Henry W. Krotzer from plans in the French National Archive. [23.2]

1726 First brickyard established at Bayou St. John.

1727 Ursuline Nuns arrived at New Orleans and established a convent and a girls' school.

1731 The Company of the Indies (formerly the Company of the West) relinquished charter and Louisiana became a crown colony; Bienville returned as governor.

New Orleans is a mere assemblage of a few poor cabins . . . made of planks and mud.
Abbé Antoine-François Prevost, *Manon Lescaut*, 1731

1734 First Ursuline Convent completed. Claude Dubreuil builder. [23.3]

First Ursuline Convent, 1734–1745, by Henry W. Krotzer from plans in the French National Archive. [23.3]

1735 First Charity Hospital established from the bequest of a French sailor.

1740 Population of New Orleans: 1,100.

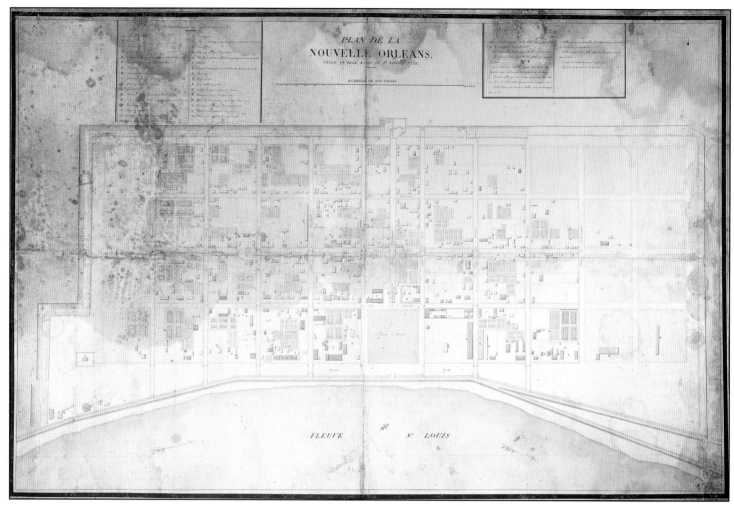

Map of New Orleans, 1732. [24.1]

1743 Pierre de Rigaud, Marquis de Vaudreuil-Cavagnal (1698–1765), succeeded Bienville as governor. Vaudreuil initiated the first serious levee system and suggested building methods appropriate to the climate and terrain of New Orleans.

Second Ursuline Convent, 1748–53. [24.2]

1748 Second Ursuline Convent begun; designed by Ignace François Broutin (d. 1751) in 1745. Claude Dubreuil builder. Completed in 1753, this is the only intact structure remaining from the French colonial period. Entrance portico added in the 1890s. [24.2]

The colonists are very proud of their capital. Suffice it to say, they sing a song in the streets here to the effect that this town is as fine a sight as Paris.
Sister Madeleine Hachard
Ursuline Convent, 1750

1754 French and Indian War began between French and English forces in America.

1760 New Orleans fortified.

1762 Louis XV gave New Orleans and the Louisiana territory west of the Mississippi to King Carlos III of Spain by secret treaty.

1763 February 6. Treaty of Paris ceded to England all French territory east of the Mississippi River and confirmed the transfer of west Louisiana to Spain.

Colonial Office built by Bernard de Verges (d. 1768). It served as the seat of government—Spanish, American, and the state of Louisiana—until it burned in 1828. [25.1]

Colonial Office, built in 1763 by Bernard de Verges. Burned in 1828. [25.1]

1764 First Acadians (Cajuns) began to arrive from Canada to settle in south Louisiana.

1768 Spain formally established its government in Louisiana under Governor Antonio de Ulloa (1716–1795). He was driven from New Orleans by a populace still sympathetic to French rule.

1769 General Don Alessandro O'Reilly (1722–1794), an Irishman in Spanish service, led 2,600 troops to quash the rebellion in New Orleans. He executed six of the rebel leaders and established Spanish government in the city.

1788 Good Friday, March 21. A great fire destroyed much of the city.

Following the fire, the first suburb, or faubourg, was subdivided outside of the original city on land first granted to Bienville, subsequently owned by the Jesuits, and finally by Marie and Bertrand Gravier. Laid out by Carlos L. Trudeau (c. 1750–1816), it was named Faubourg Ste. Marie following Madame Gravier's death.

Spanish colonists from the Canary Islands arrived.

American merchants were granted permission to trade through the port of New Orleans.

1789 St. Louis Number 1 Cemetery established. [25.2]

St. Louis Number 1 Cemetery, painted by John H. B. Latrobe in 1834. [25.2]

Construction begun on a new church, a gift of Don Andrés Almonester y Roxas; Gilberto Guillemard, architect; consecrated as St. Louis Cathedral in 1794. [25.3]

The St. Louis Cathedral in 1816. [25.3]

1791 Construction begun on the Presbytère, a rectory of the church, financed by Almonester; Guillemard was the architect; construction was halted in 1798 and completed in 1813.

Meat Market (Halle des Boucheries) built on Decatur Street.

1791 Baron Francisco Luis Hector de Carondelet (1747–1807), a native of Flanders in the Spanish service, arrived as governor and began civic improvements which included rebuilding the city's dilapidated fortifications and the introduction of street lamps. [26.1]

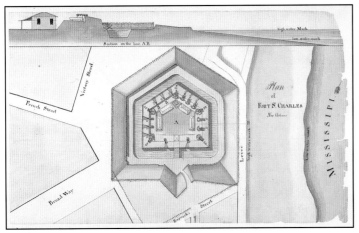

Fort St. Charles, Esplanade Avenue, drawn by Barthélémy Lafon in 1814. [26.1]

1794 Another disastrous fire razed much of the city around the Place d'Armes.

1795 A new building code for the city was drawn; wooden roofs were forbidden.

Construction started on a new Cabildo building, financed by Almonester; Guillemard, architect; completed in 1799. [26.2]

Construction begun on the Carondelet (Old Basin) Canal, between Bayou St. John and Basin Street; canal drained the back portion of the city and provided shipping access from Lake Pontchartrain; filled in between 1927 and 1938.

Pinkney's Treaty between the United States and Spain allowed American farmers in the Mississippi Valley duty-free deposit at the port of New Orleans.

1800 Louisiana retroceded to France, unbeknownst to colony.

1803 April 29. The United States agreed to purchase the Louisiana Territory from France for $15,000,000; purchase treaty signed May 2.

November 30. France took formal possession of Louisiana from Spain.

December 20. American commissioners William C. C. Claiborne (1775–1817) and General James Wilkinson (1757–1825) took formal possession of Louisiana from France for the United States in ceremonies in the Place d'Armes.

1804 Congress established the Territory of Orleans; Claiborne appointed governor and New Orleans named capital.

Place d'Armes, shown in 1803 illustration, Cabildo at left, Presbytère at right. [26.2]

New Orleans, Faubourg St. Mary, and settlement along Bayou Road. Map by Venache, 1803. [27.1]

New Orleans from the Marigny Plantation by John L. Boqueta de Woiserie in 1803. [28.1]

1805 February 22. New Orleans incorporated.

First Protestant church established, Christ Church Episcopal, on Canal at Bourbon Street.

1806 Barthélémy Lafon (1769–1820) drew plans for the subdivision of the Delord-Sarpy plantation.

Faubourg Marigny subdivided from the plantation of Bernard Xavier Philippe de Marigny de Mandeville.

1807 City Commons, the open land surrounding the Vieux Carré, given to the city by the United States government. A canal was stipulated to be constructed connecting the Mississippi to the Carondelet Canal. It was never dug and is now the site of Canal Street.

Custom House begun. Designed by Benjamin Henry Latrobe (1763–1820) and built by Robert Alexander (1781–1811). Completed in 1809. [28.2]

Custom House, 1807–09, designed by Benjamin H. Latrobe. Demolished 1820. [28.2]

1810 New Orleans population: 17,242. Louisiana population: 76,556.

Tremé plantation bought by city, combined with northern commons, and subdivided.

1811 College d'Orléans opened in Tremé as the first institution of higher learning in the state; closed in 1825.

1812 The *New Orleans* became the first steamboat to reach New Orleans.

Engine House for the New Orleans Waterworks, 1811–12, by St. Aulaire, c. 1821. [29.1]

Engine House for the New Orleans Waterworks completed. Designed by Benjamin Henry Latrobe in 1810 as part of a grand scheme for the city; Latrobe sent his son, Henry to New Orleans to oversee its construction. Latrobe's system served the city from 1822 until 1840. [29.1]

Louisiana granted statehood.

War of 1812 with England started.

1813   Meat Market rebuilt after being destroyed by a hurricane in 1812, Jacques Tanesse, architect. Between 1813 and 1866 additional structures were added to form what came to be called the French Market. The complex was greatly remodeled in the late 1930s by the WPA and again in the early 1970s. [29.2]

Meat and Vegetable Market; from 1838 illustration. [29.2]

1815   January 8. General Andrew Jackson (1767–1845) defeated British forces at the Battle of New Orleans southeast of the city; the last engagement of the War of 1812, actually fought after a peace treaty had been signed, but before it was ratified.

Louisiana State House, formerly Charity Hospital, 1815. [29.3]

Charity Hospital constructed on Canal Street; became state government house in 1828; demolished in 1849. [29.3]

1817   Henry Latrobe died of yellow fever.

1819   Benjamin Henry Latrobe arrived in New Orleans to complete the city waterworks. Redesigned tower for St. Louis Cathedral.

New Orleans . . . retains its old character without variation. The houses are, with hardly a dozen exceptions among many hundred, one-story houses. The roofs are high, covered with tiles or shingles, and project five feet over the footway. . . . These one-storied houses are very simple in their plan. The two front rooms open onto the street with French glass doors. Benjamin Henry Latrobe, *More New Orleans Notes,* March 22, 1819.

First Presbyterian Church completed; on St. Charles between Gravier and Union streets; William Brand, architect. Later known as the Strangers Church; burned in 1851. [29.4]

First Presbyterian Church, 1818–19; by St. Aulaire, c.1821. [29.4]

1820   New Orleans population: 27,176.

Louisiana State Bank, 1820; photograph c. 1930. [30.1]

1820   Louisiana State Bank built at 409 Royal Street, Benjamin Henry Latrobe, architect, Benjamin Fox, builder. This was Latrobe's last work before he died later in 1820 of yellow fever. [30.1]

1821   Artist Jean Jacques Audubon (1785–1851) set up studio in New Orleans and purchased dead birds from the French Market as subjects for his paintings.

1823   St. Louis Number 2 Cemetery established.

American Theater on Camp Street near Poydras where builder James Caldwell (1793–1863) also introduced interior and street gas lighting to New Orleans. [30.2]

American Theater, left center, and Camp Street in 1830. [30.2]

1824   New Ursuline Convent built on the site of the present Industrial Canal. [30.3]

Third Ursuline Convent, 1824. [30.3]

1825   City limits established at Felicity Street and Canal des Pêscheurs.

1826   The Mortuary Church, now Our Lady of Guadalupe Roman Catholic Church, 401 North Rampart, built to handle funerals forbidden at the St. Louis Cathedral in an attempt to prevent the spread of yellow fever. [30.4]

The Mortuary Church, 1826; photographed c. 1890 when it was St. Anthony of Padua. [30.4]

Joseph Le Carpentier (Beauregard-Keyes) house built; François Correjolles, architect.

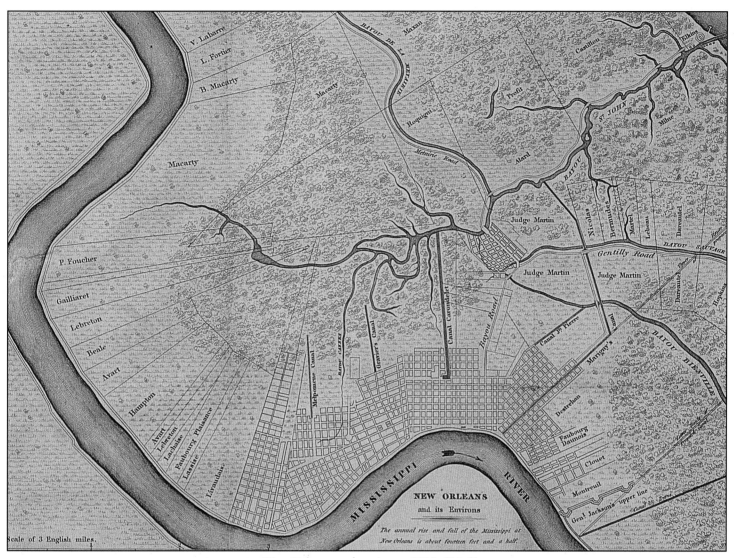

New Orleans and environs, 1829. [31.1]

1829 1,000 die of yellow fever.

1830 New Orleans population: 46,082.

State capital moved to Donaldsonville, but returned to New Orleans in 1831.

1831 Hermann house, 820 St. Louis Street built; William Brand, architect.

First railroad in New Orleans connected Faubourg Marigny and Lake Pontchartrain along Elysian Fields Avenue. Eventually part of the Louisville and Nashville Railroad, it ceased operation in 1932.

Construction started on the New Orleans Navigation (New Basin) Canal along present Pontchartrain Expressway; completed in 1835. Filled in between late 1930s and early 1950s.

1832 New Charity Hospital constructed, 1532 Tulane Avenue. [31.2]

Charity Hospital, 1832. [31.2]

1833 Faubourg Livaudais and two smaller faubourgs became the City of Lafayette.

Julia Row, 602–32 Julia Street, completed; Alexander Wood (1804–1854), architect.

New Orleans Timeline

Commercial Bank, 1832–33. [32.1]

1833 Commercial Bank completed on Magazine Street; George Clarkson (1809–1835), architect; Daniel Twogood, builder. [32.1]

It is certainly a place after its own fashion.
John H. B. Latrobe, *Journal*
November 10, 1834

1835 The largest theater in the United States, the St. Charles Theater, built, on St. Charles near Poydras; Antonio Mondelli (1799–1864), architect. Burned in 1842 and rebuilt. [32.2]

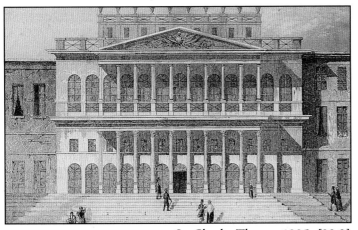

St. Charles Theater, 1835. [32.2]

The number of French and of American inhabitants is supposed to be pretty much the same; but the French predominate in the old town.
James Stuart, *Three Years in North America,* 1835

United States Mint, 1835. [32.3]

United States Mint begun, Esplanade Avenue at Decatur Street; William Strickland (1788–1854), architect. [32.3]

St. Louis Hotel begun, St. Louis Street between Royal and Chartres streets; Jacques Nicolas Bussière de Pouilly (1804–1875), architect. [32.4]

St. Louis Hotel, 1835–38. [32.4]

New Orleans and Carrollton Railroad (early St. Charles Avenue streetcar line) started service between Canal Street and Carrollton.

St. Charles Hotel begun, St. Charles Street between Common and Gravier streets; James Gallier, Sr. (1798–1866) architect. Completed in 1838, this became a center of the American community in New Orleans. [33.1]

1836 March 8. New Orleans divided into three municipalities.

St. Charles Hotel, 1835–38. [33.1]

1838 St. Patrick's Church begun on Camp Street; designed by James (1808–1852) and Charles (c. 1810–1839) Dakin, but completed by James Gallier, Sr., in 1840. [33.2]

First mention of an organized street parade of carriages on Mardi Gras.

1840 New Orleans population: 102,193; fourth largest city in the United States.

The Red Stores built, North Peters at St. Philip in the French Market; demolished by WPA in the late 1930s; replicated during the market renovation of the 1970s. [33.3]

St. Patrick's Church, 1838–40. [33.2]

The Red Stores, c. 1840. [33.3]

New Orleans Timeline

1840 Jules Lion (d. 1866), a free man of color, introduced the daguerreotype to New Orleans a few months after its introduction in Paris.

1841 Boston Club organized; named for the card game, a form of whist.

About this time the wide *batture* between Faubourg St. Mary and the river was subdivided into long, narrow blocks to accommodate large warehouses.

1842 Grid of streets laid out at Algiers Point, on the west bank of the Mississippi River across from the Vieux Carré, on the old DuVerje Plantation.

The truth is New Orleans appears to me to be at the extreme of everything. . . . Changes take place here with almost the rapidity of thought. Today rich, tomorrow poor, today well, tomorrow dead, today hot, tomorrow cold, today dry, tomorrow wet. . . . You can see here some of the richest and some of the poorest of humanity. . . . An observing man can see as much of the world and of diversified character here as in any city in the union.
Bishop Henry B. Whipple, *Southern Diary*, 1843–44

1846 Christ Episcopal Church begun on Canal Street at Dauphine Street; Thomas K. Wharton (1814–1862), architect. [36.1]

Canal Street between Burgundy and Dauphine with Christ Church and Union Terrace, 1834, a plush apartment building. Drawn by Marie Adrien Persac, 1873. [36.1]

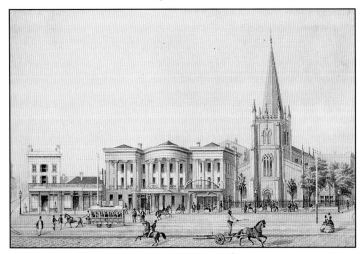

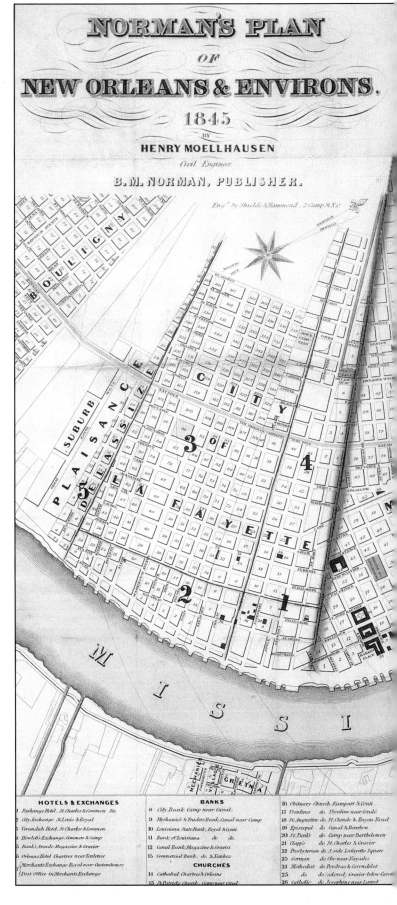

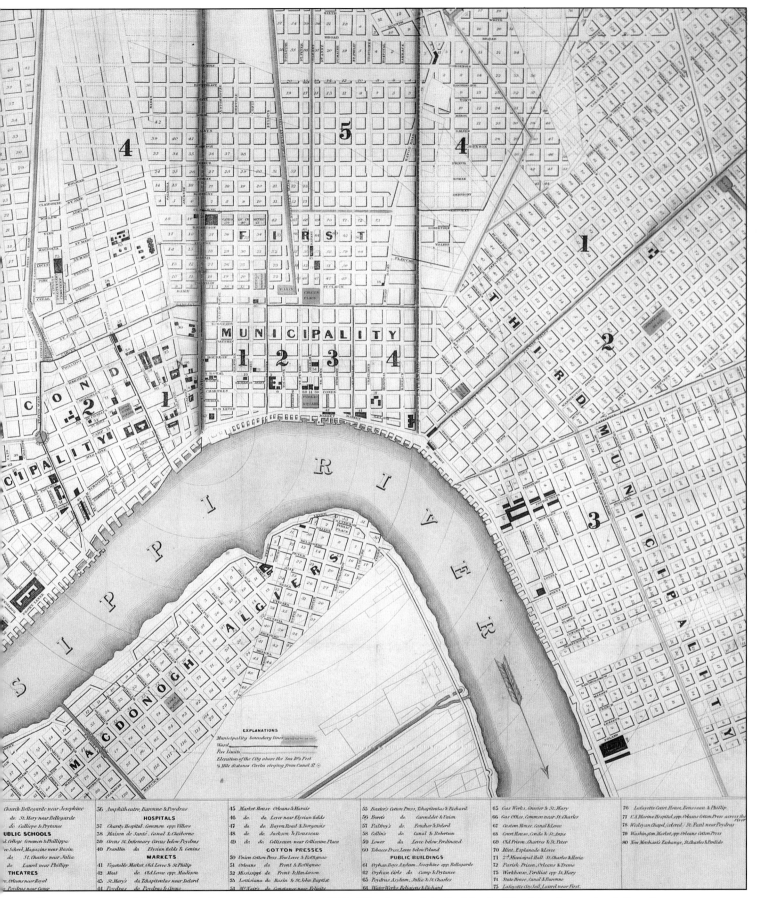

PRECEDING PAGES: *New Orleans from the west bank in 1841. The dome of the St. Charles Hotel dominates the skyline. St. Patrick's Church to the left is incorrectly shown as having a steeple.* [34.1] ABOVE: *New Orleans in 1845, showing the three municipalities, the city of Lafayette, and Algiers.* [37.1]

Designed in 1843 for the Medical College of Louisiana by James Dakin, this building was incorporated into the University of Louisiana in 1847. [38.1]

1847   The University of Louisiana established; an outgrowth of the Medical College of Louisiana, founded in 1835. [38.1]

1848   The United States Custom House begun; 423 Canal Street, the fourth customs facility on this site; Alexander T. Wood and others, architects. Completed to the roof by 1860, the cast-iron cornice was not added until 1880. [38.2]

The Custom House (1848–80) in 1873. [38.2]

1849   State capital moved to Baton Rouge.

Place d'Armes, 1849. Cathedral tower still remained as redesigned by Latrobe in 1819. [38.3]

Mansard roofs and cupolas added to the Cabildo and Presbytère. [38.3]

Pontalba Buildings begun, flanking the Place d'Armes; James Gallier, Sr., original architect; Henry Howard (1818–1884), architect of final plans.

Southern Yacht Club founded; second oldest in United States.

D. H. Holmes Dry Goods moved from Chartres to Canal Street; major retailing was beginning to leave French Quarter.

Few towns in the world possess such a medley of population. Alexander Mackay, *Travels in the United States,* 1849

1850   New Orleans population: 116,375; fifth behind New York, Philadelphia, Boston, and Baltimore.

John McDonogh (b. 1775) died and left bequest to build public school buildings.

Work began on the Touro Block of stores and offices, Canal Street; built for Judah Touro by Thomas Murray. [38.4]

Touro Block, 1850–57; by Marie Adrien Persac in 1873. [38.4]

1851 Place d'Armes redesigned under the plans of Baroness Micaëla Pontalba (1794–1874) and renamed Jackson Square.

St. Louis Cathedral essentially rebuilt; Jacques de Pouilly, architect.

St. Charles Hotel burned; rebuilt without a dome; George Purves (d. 1883), architect. [39.1]

Second St. Charles Hotel, 1851; photograph c. 1858. [39.1]

One section of New Orleans, the First Municipality, is the old city; in the Second Municipality, the new city, here is a little of Boston, there is a trifle of New York, and some of Philadelphia, with something of the rus in urbe so charmingly common to New England towns. The third section [is] a species of half village, half city (unmistakable in its French Faubourg look).
A. Oakey Hall, *The Manhattaner in New Orleans*, 1851

1852 The three municipalities reunited. City of Lafayette annexed.

1853 Yellow fever killed 8,000 citizens.

City Hall, on right, 1845–53; photograph c. 1858. [39.2]

City Hall (Second Municipality Hall, now Gallier Hall) dedicated, 545 St. Charles Avenue; construction began in 1845; James Gallier, Sr., architect. [39.2]

1854 Judah Touro died; his estate offered money for the paving and beautification of Canal Street; completed in 1859. [39.3]

Repaving Canal Street; view c. 1858, from Custom House. [39.3]

Carrollton Courthouse begun; Henry Howard, architect. Completed in 1855.

1855 Construction begun on Ecclesiastical Square, a complex of churches, schools, and associated structures of the Redemptorest Fathers to serve the various ethnic groups; completed in 1860s. [39.4]

Ecclesiastical Square, on Constance Street, 1855–60s; St. Mary's Assumption (German language) is on the left and St. Alphonsus (Irish English) is on the right. [39.4]

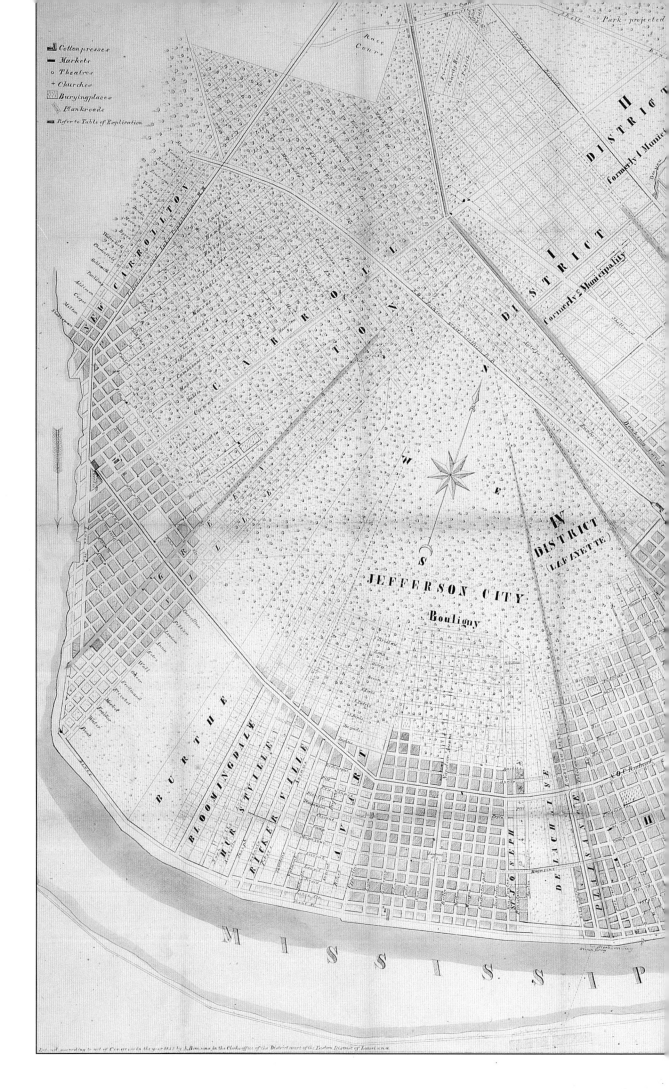

Cottonpresses
Markets
Theatres
Churches
Buryingplaces
Plankroads
Refer to Table of Explication

PLAN
OF
NEW ORLEANS
and
ENVIRONS

new original Delineation by W. Walter.

published by A. Bronsema
Camp Str. No 74.
1855.

New Orleans Timeline

Jackson Square in mid-1850s, flanked by Pontalba Buildings and showing rebuilt St. Louis Cathedral and Jackson Monument. [42.1]

1856   Equestrian statue of Andrew Jackson by Clark Mills (1815–1883) unveiled in Jackson Square. Statue is a replica of one by Mills in Washington, D. C. [42.1]

First Presbyterian Church built on site of earlier church at Lafayette Square; Henry Howard, architect; George Purves, builder. [42.2]

1857   James Robb (1814–1881) built largest private house in New Orleans; James Gallier, Jr. (1827–1868), architect. Later housed Newcomb College.

Church of the Immaculate Conception, 132 Baronne Street, opened. Rebuilt 1927–28.

First parade of the Mistick Krewe of Comus, the first carnival organization. [42.3]

Mistick Krewe of Comus parade, Mardi Gras 1867. [42.3]

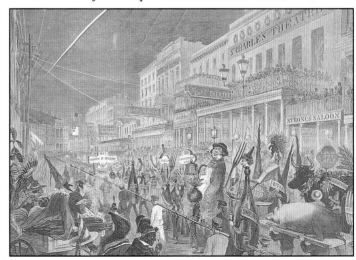

First Presbyterian Church, 1855–56, at Lafayette Square. [42.2]

Architect James Gallier, Jr., built his home at 1132 Royal Street.

St. Anna's Asylum built at 1823 Prytania Street by the Society for the Relief of Destitute Females and their Helpless Children; Robert Little and Peter Middlemiss, builders. [43.1]

St. Anna's Asylum, 1857. [43.1]

The first feeling on entering New Orleans is that you are in a city differing from all others in the Union. Even the American quarter has borrowed and adapted the old French architecture, although now and then you come upon one of those enormities in the shape of a porticoed dwelling-house peculiar to New England.
William Kingsford, *Impressions of the West and South,* Toronto, 1858

1859 French Opera House opened at Bourbon and Toulouse streets; James Gallier, Jr., and Richard Esterbrook, architects. Burned in 1919. [43.2]

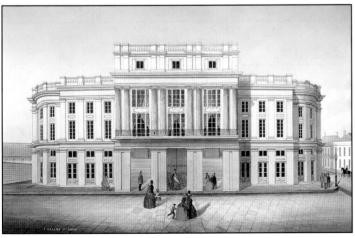

French Opera House, 1859; painting by Marie Adrien Persac. [43.2]

1860 New Orleans population: 168,675.

Have you ever been to New Orleans? If not you'd better go, . . . It's a nation of a queer place; day and night a show!
Colonel James R. Creecy, *Scenes in the South,* 1860

Henry Clay Monument on Canal Street at Royal and St. Charles dedicated; an important central gathering place until it was removed to Lafayette Square in 1901.

1861 January 26. Louisiana seceded from the Union and joined the Confederacy.

1862 April 30. City surrendered to Admiral David G. Farragut and on May 1 was placed under the Federal rule of General Benjamin F. (Beast) Butler.

Judah P. Benjamin (1811–1880) of New Orleans appointed Confederate Secretary of State.

1864 May 11. Slavery abolished in Louisiana by constitutional amendment.

1866 The Bazaar Market built; the only French Market structure with cupolas. [43.3]

The Bazaar Market, 1866. [43.3]

1868 Louisiana readmitted to Union under Reconstruction government.

1869 Construction started on St. Joseph's Roman Catholic Church; completed 1893.

1869 Union Normal Teachers College and Straight University founded, both for African-American students. They later merged to form Dillard University.

St. John the Baptist, 1869–72. [44.1]

Cornerstone laid for Church of St. John the Baptist, Dryades Street; Albert Diettel (1824–1896), architect; Thomas Mulligan, builder; building dedicated in 1872. [44.1]

1870 New Orleans population: 191,418.

Twelfth Night Revelers organized.

New Orleans, Mobile, and Chattanooga Railroad completed, later part of Louisville and Nashville.

Algiers and Jefferson City annexed.

1871 New Orleans Cotton Exchange organized.

Land purchased for the Upper City Park, renamed Audubon Park in 1886.

Leland University founded for African-American students.

New Orleans flood of 1871. [44.2]

Flood covered much of the city. [44.2]

Belknap Fountain erected on Canal Street, later moved to City Park. [44.3]

Canal Street between Camp and St. Charles; drawn in 1873 by Marie Adrien Persac. Belknap Fountain at left. Fifth building from right, 622 Canal (1859), is one of the finest surviving examples of a cast-iron façade in New Orleans. [44.3]

1872 First Rex, King of Carnival, with Mardi Gras colors of purple, green, and gold and the song, "If Ever I Cease to Love."

Paul Morphy (1837–1884), of New Orleans, published *Games of Chess.*

French artist Edgar Degas arrived in New Orleans to stay with his relatives.

Metairie Cemetery established on site of Metairie Race Track.

Fair Grounds Race Track established.

1874 Carrollton annexed.

1875 Mardi Gras declared a legal holiday in New Orleans.

1876 First telephone in New Orleans.

1877 Reconstruction ended; Federal troops withdrawn.

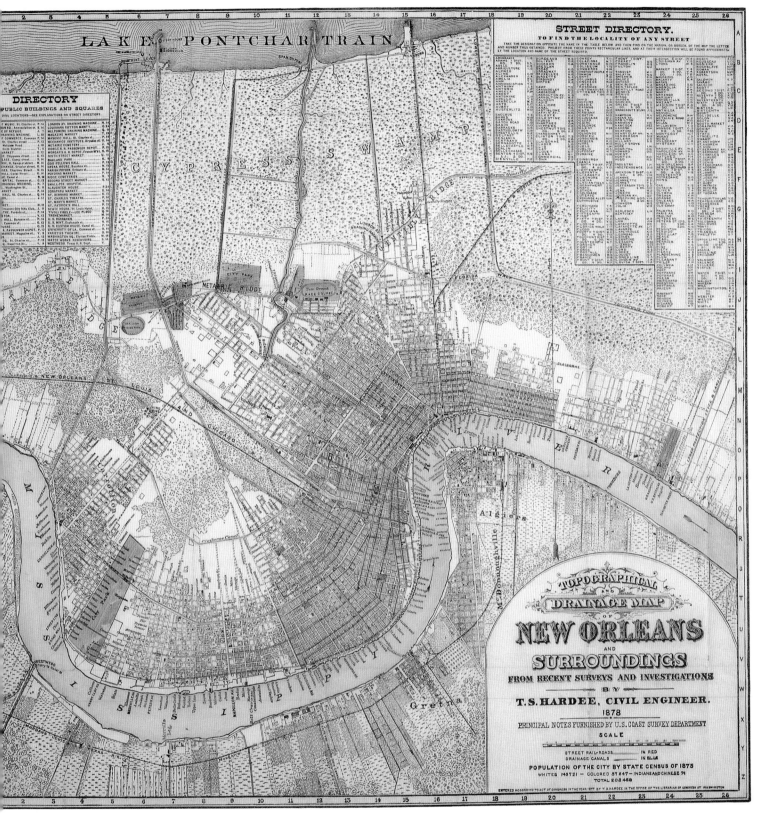

New Orleans, 1878. [45.1]

1878 Second worst yellow fever epidemic in city resulted in nearly 5,000 deaths, bringing about quarantine of city and a growing demand for improvement of sanitary conditions.

1879 James Eads Jetties completed; designed to prevent siltation at the mouth of the Mississippi. The channel was deepened, which allowed large ships access to the port of New Orleans.

THE WORLD'S INDUSTRIAL AND COTTON CENTENNIAL EXPOSITION.
MAIN BUILDING.   GOVERNMENT BLDG.
HORTICULTURAL BLDG.   ART GALLERY.
FACTORY AND MILLS.

Bayou Metairie
· Mississippi Valley R.R.

Bayou Poydras   St.John's Ch.
St.Alphonsus Church.   Temple Sinai.
Church.St.Mary's Assumption.   Lee Monument.
                                  Annunciation Square.

West End.
(Lake Pontchartrain.)

1st Presb
St.Patrick's C

COPYRIGHT

THE CITY OF
AND THE MISSISSIPPI RIVER

Cotton Exchange.   Christ Church.   Bayou St.John   Congo Sq.   Spanish Fort   Opera House.   French Cathedral   French Market   U.S.Mint
Square.   Jesuit Ch.and College. Pickwick Club.   Hotel Royal   Sugar Exchange   Jackson Square   Morgan Ferry
     St.Charles Hotel   Canal St.   Post Office and Custom Ho   Depot Louisville & Nashville RR.   Sugar and Cotton Sheds   LEVEE.   ALGIERS

NEW ORLEANS,

E PONTCHARTRAIN IN DISTANCE.

1880 New Orleans population: 216,090.

1881 Work started on the asphalt paving of St. Charles Avenue; completed in 1885. At the time it was the largest asphalt paving project in the world.

Electric lighting introduced to New Orleans.

1882 The state capital was permanently located in Baton Rouge.

First Krewe of Proteus parade.

1883 Mark Twain's *Life on the Mississippi* published.

Pickwick Club built, Canal and Carondelet streets; N. C. Hinsdale and Oliver Marble, architects. Building demolished 1949. [48.1]

Elaborate new Cotton Exchange Building constructed at the corner of Carondelet and Gravier streets; Henry Wolters, architect. [48.2]

1884 World's Industrial and Cotton Centennial Exposition opened in Upper City (Audubon) Park. All buildings were taken down except for the Horticultural Hall, which was lost in the 1915 hurricane.

Robert E. Lee Monument, 1884. [48.3]

Robert E. Lee Monument dedicated in Place du Tivoli (now Lee Circle); statue by Alexander Doyle, column by John Roy. [48.3]

University of Louisiana became Tulane University after a donation from Paul Tulane (1801–1887).

The vast area covered by the city is almost as flat as a billiard-board . . . in every direction it is intersected with street railways such as are universal in American towns . . . but which are said to have been first introduced in New Orleans.
The Rev. David Macre, *The Americans at Home*, 1885

1886 Mercier Building constructed, Canal and Dauphine streets; William Freret (1833–1911), architect. [see 51.1]

ABOVE: Canal Street at St. Charles. Pickwick Club building is at far right. Henry Clay Monument, 1860, at center. Crescent Billiard Hall at left; 1875 remodeling by Henry Howard and Frederick Wing. [48.1] BELOW: Cotton Exchange, 1883. [48.2]

Sophie Newcomb College for Girls established.

1887 Construction begun on Howard Library, 615 Howard Avenue; designed by the Boston firm of Shepley, Rutan, & Coolidge; conception by Henry Hobson, Richardson (1838–1886), a nationally known architect who grew up nearby at Julia Row. Library opened in 1889.[49.1]

Howard Library, 1887–89. [49.1]

1888 I. L. Lyons (Gravier) Building constructed on Gravier Street; D. W. Kendall, architect. The eight-story warehouse was called a "skyscraper" at the time. [49.2]

I. L. Lyons Building, 1888. [49.2]

New Orleans is the most cosmopolitan of provincial cities. Its comparative isolation has secured the development of provincial traits and manners, has preserved the individuality of the many races that give it color, morals, and character, while its close relations with France, and the constant influx of Northern men of business and affairs, have given it the air of a metropolis.
Charles Dudley Warner, *Harper's New Monthly Magazine,* January 1887

1889 December 6. Jefferson Davis died while visiting friends in the Garden District.

Morris Building (former Cigali Building, another early "skyscraper" type) constructed, 600 Canal Street; Thomas Sully (1855–1939), architect. [see 51.2]

1890 New Orleans population: 242,039.

1891 City Park Improvement Association formed to develop the Allard tract at Bayou Metairie, the nucleus of City Park.

1892 James J. ("Gentleman Jim") Corbett defeated John L. Sullivan at the Olympic Club, Royal Street. New Orleans was a leading venue for professional boxing in the United States.

1893 Large criminal courthouse constructed on site of present main library at Loyola Avenue; Maxamillion Orloop, architect. [49.3]

Criminal Courthouse, 1893. [49.3]

New Orleans Timeline

1893 Electric streetcars introduced on St. Charles line; this accelerated growth in uptown and Carrollton neighborhoods.

1894 Construction begun on the first buildings on the St. Charles Avenue campus of Tulane University; Andry and Bendernagel, architects. [50.1]

Richardson Memorial Building, built in 1908. Originally housed the Tulane Medical School, now the Tulane School of Architecture. [50.1]

City house numbering system converted and simplified to system now in use.

Second St. Charles Hotel burned and rebuilt; Thomas Sully, architect. Demolished in 1974. [50.2]

The third St. Charles Hotel, 1894. Painting by Oscar Griffith, c. 1916. [50.2]

Hennen Building, 1895; renovated 1922. [50.3]

1895 Hennen (Maritime) Building constructed, 201–11 Carondelet Street; the first ten-story building in New Orleans; Thomas Sully, architect. [50.3]

The Crescent City has most of the features of a true capital and metropolis. . . . It is par excellence *a city of fun, fair women, rich food, and flowers.*
Julian Ralph, *Dixie, or Southern Scenes and Sketches,* 1896

1896 Board of Commissioners of the Port of New Orleans (Port Authority) established.

Sewerage and Water Board established as an outgrowth of New Orleans Drainage Commission.

1897 City Council passed ordinance establishing the Storyville "red-light" district. Closed in 1917.

First yellow fever epidemic in nearly two decades broke out.

Mercier Building on Canal Street at Dauphine became the Maison Blanche Department Store. Demolished in 1906 for new Maison Blanche building. [51.1]

Maison Blanche (Mercier Building) in 1899, built in 1886. [51.1]

Canal Street beautified and paved with asphalt.

1900 New Orleans population: 287,104; twelfth largest city in the United States.

Morris Building burned; renovated with the addition of bay windows and a deep cornice. [51.2]

Morris Building, 1889, renovated after 1900 fire. [51.2]

Port Authority took over the operation of the port; construction begun soon after on large covered warehouses.

1901 Oil discovered in Louisiana near Jennings.

Civil Courts Building, 1907–09. [51.3]

1907 Civil Courts Building started at 400 Royal Street in an attempt to upgrade a declining French Quarter; Frederick W. Brown, A. Ten Eyck Brown (1878–1940), and P. Thornton Marye (1872–1935), associated architects; completed in 1909. [51.3]

Water purification plant completed.

Hibernia Bank (Carondelet Building), 214 Carondelet Street built; Charles Allen Favrot (1866–1939) and Louis Adolph Livaudais (d. 1932), architects.

Monteleone Hotel, 214 Royal Street built; Albert Toledano (1858–1923) and Victor Wogan (b. 1870), architects.

Southern Railway Station built on Canal Street; Daniel H. Burnham (1846–1912), architect. Opened 1908.

Business here is absorbing everything, as it is everywhere in the South. Soon it will overrun and change much, if not all, in the physical aspect, as well as the social life, of the Crescent City, which in former times distinguished the place from all other American communities. The rising tide of business that is even now roaring through Canal Street, is beating against the boundaries of that old picturesque French Quarter.
Charles Morris, *The Old South and the New,* 1907

1908 Grunewald (Roosevelt, Fairmont) Hotel built, 118–140 University Place; Toledano and Wogan, architects.

New Orleans Timeline

Public Library, 1908. [52.1]

1908   Public Library built on St. Charles at Lee Circle; Collins Diboll, Sr. (1863–1936), and Allison Owen (1869–1919), architects. Demolished 1959. [52.1]

1909   First Zulu Mardi Gras parade.

Canal Street, c. 1922; new Maison Blanche Building, 1909, is the large building at left center. [52.2]

Maison Blanche Building completed at Canal and Dauphine streets, replacing the Mercier Building; Stone Brothers, architects. [52.2]

The Delgado Museum of Art, now the New Orleans Museum of Art, in City Park. [52.3]

Delgado Museum of Art design competition held, won by Lebenbaum and Marx. Built in 1911, became New Orleans Museum of Art in 1971. [52.3]

1910   New Orleans population: 339,075.

1911   Whitney Bank built, St. Charles Avenue and Gravier Street; Clinton and Russell, architects, in association with Emile Weil. [52.4]

Whitney National Bank, 1911. [52.4]

Construction begun on the St. Charles Avenue campus of Loyola Academy, incorporated as Loyola University in 1912.

1912   New Ursuline Convent constructed, 2635 State Street.

1913   American Institute of Architects national convention held in New Orleans.

1914   Audubon Park Commission formed.

1915   September 29. Severe hurricane struck city causing heavy damage.

Post Office completed on Camp Street at Lafayette Square; Hale and Rogers, architects. [53.1]

Post Office, 1915. [53.1]

Administration Building, 1932, Xavier University. [53.2]

Cotton Exchange, 1921. [53.3]

Hibernia Bank Building, 1921. [53.4]

1916 Xavier University founded; the only historically Black, Catholic university in the United States. [53.2]

1919 Orpheum Theater built, 129 University Place.

1920 New Orleans population: 378,219.

1921 New Cotton Exchange built on the site of the old exchange; Charles Allen Favrot and Louis Adolph Livaudais, architects. [53.3]

Hibernia Bank Building completed; Favrot and Livaudais, architects. At twenty-three stories and 355 feet, this was the tallest building in New Orleans for more than forty years. [53.4]

1922 Writer Sherwood Anderson moved to the French Quarter, where a number of writers and artists began to settle. At that time there also began a growing interest in historic preservation.

New Orleans Timeline

Bird's-eye view of the Central Business District, looking toward the river, c. 1922. [54.1]

I am living in an old house in the old Creole section of New Orleans, surely the most civilized spot in America. The houses and the people, Italians, French Creoles, and Negroes, are charmingly unambitious, basically cultured, and gentle.
Sherwood Anderson, in a letter from New Orleans, 1922

1923 Le Petit Théâtre du Vieux Carré built, St. Peter and Chartres streets; Armstrong and Koch, architects.

Inner Harbor Navigation Canal (Industrial Canal) completed; connected Lake Pontchartrain with the Mississippi River. [54.2]

Dedication of the Industrial Canal, May 5, 1923. [54.2]

1927 Canal Bank (First National Bank of Commerce) built on Baronne Street; Emile Weil, architect. [54.3]

Baronne Street: Pere Marquette Building, 1925, left; Canal Bank, 1927, center; Union Indemnity Building, 1924, right. [54.3]

American (Alerion) Bank Building, 1928–29. [55.1]

1928 American (Alerion) Bank Building begun; Moise Goldstein (c 1882–1972), architect. [55.1]

Lakefront reclamation begun, completed in the early 1930s.

1929 Stock market crash marked the end of a commercial building surge in the Central Business District that began in the 1880s.

Repaving and beautification of Canal Street begun; present light standards installed.

1930 Municipal Auditorium opened; Favrot and Livaudais, architects. [55.2]

Municipal Auditorium, 1930. [55.2]

New Orleans population: 458,762.

1934 Louisiana portion of Historic American Buildings Survey (HABS) begun in New Orleans.

1935 January 1. First Sugar Bowl played; Tulane 21, Temple 14.

WPA (Work Projects Administration) established; in the late 1930s undertook renovation of the French Market. [55.3]

WPA renovation of the French Market in the late 1930s. [55.3]

Dillard University campus formally opened on Gentilly Boulevard; Moise Goldstein, campus architect.

Shushan (Lakefront) Airport opened; Leon Charles Weiss, Felix Julius Dreyfous, and Solis Seiferth, architects.

Bonnet Carré Spillway dedicated.

Huey P. Long Bridge completed upriver from New Orleans. [55.4]

Dedication of the Huey P. Long Bridge, 1935. [55.4]

New Orleans Timeline

1936 Vieux Carré Commission authorized by state.

Sensing its own individuality, deeply rooted in the past, the City has sought to preserve its way of life, which it considers good. The traditions, the subtle influence of Spanish and French background, have had their conscious and unconscious effects.
George M. Reynolds, *Politics in New Orleans*, 1936

A city architecturally unique in this country . . . [but] like all cities, in all times, New Orleans has its share of ugliness along with its beauty, poverty along with its well-being, depravity along with its virtue . . . [but] the lasting impression is that made . . . by the finer things.
Editors, *"Pencil Points,"* 1938

1938 Playwright Tennessee Williams lived in New Orleans briefly; returned in the 1940s on a more permanent basis.

1939 Charity Hospital built, 1532 Tulane Avenue; Solis Seiferth, architect. [56.1]

Charity Hospital, 1939. [56.1]

1940 New Orleans population: 494,537.

New Orleans is a very big city and quite lovely. The old French Quarter is far bigger and better than I thought it would be. Really picturesque.
Henry Miller, in letters to Anais Nin, 1941

1942 Edgar and Edith Rosenwald Stern completed Longue Vue; opened to the public in 1968.

New Orleans isn't like other cities.
Stella Kowalski, *A Streetcar Named Desire*, by Tennessee Williams, 1947

Much is written about the famous and unique charm of New Orleans; it is not so commonly realized that, in actual essence, it is a tough dockyard city.
John Gunther, *Inside USA*, 1947

Romantic New Orleans, picturesque New Orleans, carefree New Orleans. . . . We feel like saying, in our determination not to be taken in, that no place . . . could be as romantic, picturesque, and as carefree as that!
Hamilton Basso, *A New Orleans Reader*, 1948

Canal Street and Central Business District, 1948. [56.2]

1949 Loyola Avenue created to facilitate traffic movement from the uptown area to the Central Business District.

1950 New Orleans population: 570,445; metropolitan population: 685,000.

Skyline of Central Business District, 1954. [57.1]

1957   New City Hall dedicated; Goldstein, Parham, and Labouisse, in association with Favrot, Reed, Mathes, and Bergiman, architects.

Lake Pontchartrain Causeway opened; the longest bridge in the world.

1958   The Greater New Orleans Mississippi River Bridge completed.

Louisiana State University at New Orleans established; later renamed the University of New Orleans.

Pontchartrain Expressway built on the route of the filled-in New Basin Canal. [57.2]

Pontchartrain Expressway, [57.2]

1960 New Orleans population: 627,525; metropolitan population: 907,000.

Royal Orleans Hotel built on site of old St. Louis Hotel, 501 St. Louis Street; plan by Nathaniel Curtis and Arthur Q. Davis, exterior by Richard Koch and Samuel Wilson, Jr.

Lakeside Shopping Center built.

It was neither the Creole tradition nor the American tradition that built up the New Orleans of today, but a blending of both in which each is indebted to the other, as New Orleans is indebted to both.
Sean O'Faolain, *"New Orleans," Holiday,* 1961

225 Baronne Building, 1962, top left center, photographed c. 1970. [58.1]

1962 225 Baronne Building completed; at twenty-eight stories and 362 feet, it was the first structure to exceed the 1921 Hibernia Bank Building in height; Shaw Metz and Associates, architects. [58.1]

Post Office and Federal Building complex built at 701 Loyola Avenue.

1963 Poydras Street widening begun.

1965 Hurricane Betsy struck the city.

The International Trade Mart, 1966, center, and Plaza Tower, 1966, top left, were prominent additions to the skyline. [58.2]

1966 International Trade Mart completed; Edward Stone and Robert Lee Hall and Associates, architects. [58.2]

Plaza Tower built, forty-five stories and 531 feet; the city's tallest building at the time; Leonard Spangenberg, architect. [58.2]

The work of current New Orleans architects is to be criticized, not because it falls below some national average, but because, with such a splendid tradition, it does not rise above it.
James Marston Fitch, *Creole Architecture, 1718–1860: The Rise and Fall of a Great Tradition,* 1968

1969 First Bacchus parade held.

July 1. Transportation Secretary John A. Volpe cancelled the Vieux Carré Riverfront Expressway, stating: "It would have seriously impaired the historic quality of New Orleans' famed French Quarter."

1974 Preservation Resource Center founded.

Piazza D'Italia design competition won by Charles W. Moore.

1975 Louisiana Superdome completed, 1300 Poydras Street. Design begun in 1967 as a joint venture among numerous firms of architects and engineers; construction started in 1971. [59.2]

Louisiana Superdome, 1971–75. [59.2]

1978 Three downtown historic districts designated along with a Central Business District historic district to administer them.

1980 New Orleans population: 557,482; metropolitan area: 1,256,668.

1970 New Orleans population: 591,520; metropolitan population exceeds 1,000,000 for the first time.

1971 One Shell Square completed, fifty-one stories and 697 feet; the city's tallest building; Skidmore, Owings, & Merrill, architects. The Central Business District entered a major building boom that would dramatically transform the skyline during the next fifteen years. [59.1]

Construction of One Shell Square, 1971. [59.1]

The modern New Orleans business district dwarfs the old city, to the right, marked by the spires of the St. Louis Cathedral. [60.1]

1983   Windsor Court Hotel opened; recognized as one of the world's finest.

1984   Louisiana World Exposition opened. Convention Center served as one of the fair pavilions, and the fair helped bring about the revitalization of the Warehouse District.

Jax Brewery reopened as a retail center on Decatur Street.

1985   Place St. Charles built on the site of the St. Charles Hotel.

1986   The Riverwalk retail center opened in the old Poydras Street Wharf.

1988   Roof of the Cabildo burned. Immediate restoration undertaken by architect Samuel Wilson, Jr., and others.

New Orleans Centre retail complex opened next to the Superdome, anchored by Macy's and Lord and Taylor.

The second span of the Greater New Orleans Mississippi River Bridge opened and was named the Crescent City Connection.

1989   The Canal Street store of D. H. Holmes, one of the oldest retail enterprises in the city, closed. The property was donated to the city for redevelopment.

1990 New Orleans population: 496,938; metropolitan population: 1,238,816; city population showed significant decline while metropolitan remained stable.

The Aquarium of the Americas opened on the riverfront at the French Quarter.

1991 "Live in a Landmark" program initiated by the Preservation Resource Center to encourage and assist in the purchase and restoration of historic neighborhood houses.

Eccentric, Authentic New Orleans.
Padgett Powell, *New York Times Magazine*, 1992

1992 Construction of a new mansard roof and cupola begun on the Cabildo.

Louisiana state legislature approved establishement of a single, land-based casino to be built in New Orleans.

1993 Renovation of the Wildlife and Fisheries Building on Royal Street begun to house the Louisiana State Supreme Court.

This city moves at its own pace. People here are natural storytellers. They really are spiritual, in a Catholic sense. They really do care more about a good cup of coffee than mowing the grass.
Anne Rice, *Playboy "Interview,"* 1993

New Orleans Timeline

GAZETTEER:
Classic New Orleans Neighborhoods

"CLASSIC" NEW ORLEANS is an elusive concept hidden within the history of her distinctive neighborhoods. To appreciate it one must recognize the influences crucial to the city's evolution: that geography forced early expansion to hug the banks of the river; that early faubourgs were settled according to cultural backgrounds; that New Orleans was one of the great cities of the world in the middle of the nineteenth century; and that the assimilation of its culturally diverse qualities eventually determined its unique eclectic character.

Visitors to the city today should keep in mind that this famous and historic metropolis was once a subtropical jungle surrounded by bayous and swamps and barely adequate for human habitation. For decades after its settlement, the remote outpost of La Nouvelle-Orléans grew slowly, but near the end of the eighteenth century, as trade down the Mississippi increased, the population began to exceed the capacity of the original plan. Expansion beyond the fortified town limits was dictated by the amount and location of high ground suitable for building. Vast plantations adjoined the old town, but their arable land did not extend very far back from the Mississippi toward Lake Pontchartrain before declining into great cypress swamps. Therefore, as the plantation owners subdivided their lands into faubourgs for development and speculation, the growth of the city tended to follow the banks of the river. Upriver (away from the Gulf) and downriver (toward the Gulf) are still principal directional terms in New Orleans. Only after the invention of mechanical pumps and the implementation of a system of canals, sluices, pumping stations, and man-made levees was the city able to drain and fill the swamps and subdivide much of the incorporated area.

The age-old inclination for people of similar cultural backgrounds to congregate determined original neighborhood patterns and influenced later development. Since the landscape forced New Orleans to grow first in a linear fashion along the Mississippi, this tendency was heightened, with Anglo-Americans generally settling in faubourgs upriver and French and Creoles in the Vieux Carré and downriver faubourgs. As the city grew, new ethnic groups migrated into the pattern with their own influences.

When the Louisiana Territory and the so-called Isle of Orleans were purchased by the United States in 1803, the city consisted of only two basic sections: the original settlement, now called the Vieux Carré, or French Quarter; and an upriver suburb, Faubourg Ste. Marie, dating from 1788 and eventually the center of American development. Together they formed the classic nucleus of New Orleans. The approximately 8,000 people living in the city in 1803 were a varied group, but principally French, Spanish, Anglo-American, African-American slaves, and free persons of color. By 1810 the population had more than doubled, to 17,242, and most of the increase could be attributed to the massive immigration of people fleeing the slave revolt in Santo Domingo. In the next twenty years the population increased by nearly 30,000 more, to 46,082, as waves of Americans along with Irish and German immigrants joined the multicultural community. The growth of the following decade was even more remarkable, and in 1840 New Orleans was the fourth largest city in the nation, with more than 100,000 inhabitants.

The city had incorporated in 1805, but by 1836, disagreements between the three principal sections of the city were so intense the city charter was abrogated, and three municipalities were formed, each with its own council. The First Municipality contained the Vieux Carré, and the Third extended to St. Bernard Parish and included the Faubourg Marigny. These comprised the French and Creole section of the city. The Second Municipality was the American Sector, Faubourg Ste. Marie, which was angli-

Madame John's Legacy, Vieux Carré, in 1891.

cized to St. Mary. Populated by aggressive entrepreneurs, Faubourg St. Mary soon became the center of commerce and new wealth.

The unwieldy system of separate municipalities lasted until 1852, when a new charter was drawn reuniting the city under one government with four districts—three corresponding to the three municipalities and the fourth being the former city of Lafayette, upriver from Faubourg St. Mary. In 1870 Algiers, across the river, and the upriver city of Jefferson were added as the Fifth and Sixth districts. Carrollton, even farther upriver, was annexed into the city as the Seventh District in 1874, completing the incorporation of the current city configuration, which coincides with that of Orleans Parish, an area of 199 square miles. In 1874 about ninety percent was still swampland, and even today much of eastern New Orleans is undeveloped.

The history of the evolution from plantations to independent faubourgs and small municipalities to modern neighborhoods is at once fascinating and complex. Contemporary New Orleans is a city of strongly independent neighborhoods, each with its own cultural, economic, and architectural characteristics. A proper appreciation of the city requires a recognition of how these neighborhoods have evolved and how they fit into the overall city fabric. Unfortunately, through the years many things have happened to cloud the issue. For one, neighborhood names have changed. During the early nineteenth century people often referred to their neighborhoods by the names of towns subdivided from plantations. By mid-century they more often associated themselves with districts or political wards. Second, nineteenth-century neighborhoods were sometimes known by ethnic descriptions, such as "Little Saxony" and "Irish Channel," the latter of which is still in use. Conversely, some historic district designations, such as Bywater, are modern terms and did not exist in the nineteenth century. Most significantly, traditional neighborhoods and historic districts of the same names do not necessarily share the same boundaries, since many of the old names still in use often had broader meanings with no intention and no need of being precise. The Garden District, for example,

sometimes referred to fashionable uptown neighborhoods in general, rather than the area specifically described by the historic district of the same name. The intent of this gazetteer is to render comprehensible this network of neighborhoods and how it fits together to form the *tout ensemble* of classic New Orleans.

One key to understanding is the recognition of residential building types and trends and how they relate to the culture and chronology of neighborhood development. The classic patterns which characterize the traditional domestic architecture of New Orleans date from several periods, having evolved in various districts and neighborhoods where particular house or building types predominated. For example, colonial, Creole styles are common in the older areas such as the French Quarter and nearby Creole suburbs, while concentrations of Greek Revival façades are more obvious in the mid-nineteenth-century Garden and Lower Garden districts. New Orleans is a city without absolutes, however, and examples from almost every size and style may be found throughout the city.

The early floor plans were without halls, typical of the French colonial plantation house, the Creole cottage, and later, the shotgun cottage. In time, raised, center-hall villas became popular in the suburbs and side-hall townhouses, sometimes built over ground-floor storefronts, were favored in the Vieux Carré and the urban areas of the early adjacent faubourgs. New Orleanians made composites of these types and styles, and they adapted national trends to suit their local tastes and climate.

The people of New Orleans began sheltering themselves with characteristic style in the eighteenth century in patterns well established by the mid-nineteenth. Suitably and interestingly, oftentimes delightfully and imaginatively, and sometimes richly and uniquely, generations have built homes in distinctive districts throughout this extraordinary city. Assisted by talented architects and engineers, builders and craftsmen, landscape architects and gardeners, interior decorators and antiquarians, and decorative and fine artists, they have created a livable, lively, and original town that is unmistakably itself.

Faubourg St. Mary, c. 1842, showing the St. Charles Hotel dome.

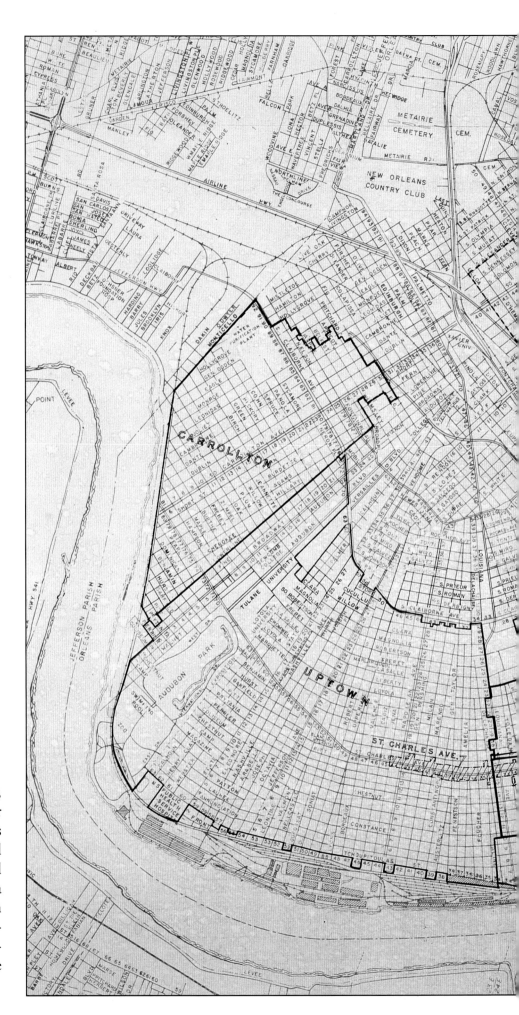

For convenience and consistency, district designations in the gazetteer coincide with those indicated on this map. They are arranged in a general chronological order and geographical direction, beginning with the area first laid out by Adrien de Pauger in 1721. Examples of classic New Orleans house-types and floor plans accompany districts in which they are commonly found.

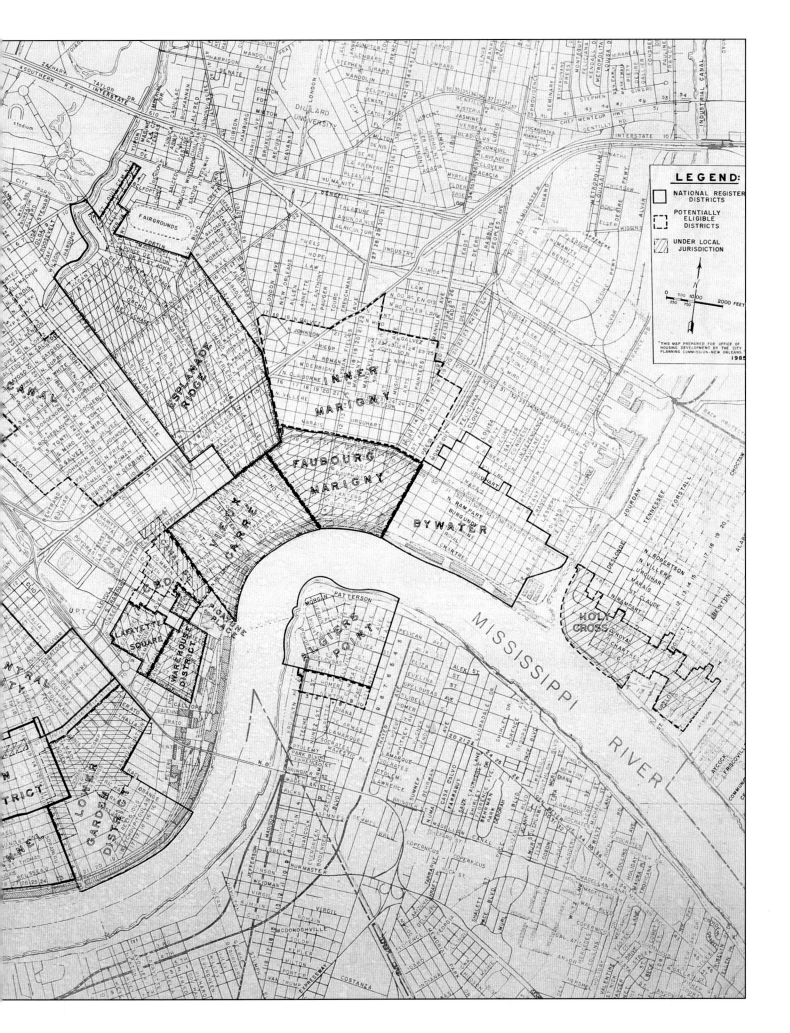

Neighborhoods Gazetteer

ABOVE: *Chartres Street at Governor Nicholls Street, looking toward the Central Business District, 1992. [66.1]* BELOW: *Madame John's Legacy, on Dumaine Street, around 1890. [66.2]*

BELOW: *A conceptual rendering of the 1792 Merieult house, now part of the Historic New Orleans Collection complex, illustrated in a nineteenth-century setting by Boyd Cruise. [66.3]*

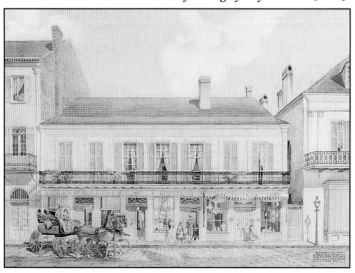

The Vieux Carré

The Vieux Carré district was, for almost seventy years, the entire town of La Nouvelle-Orléans. Its modern boundaries, Canal Street, Rampart Street, and Esplanade Avenue, form the approximate outlines of the original city. After a time, the town was fortified, and beyond the ramparts was a buffer area, or commons, developed during the Spanish period for increased security. Vieux Carré, meaning Old Square, refers to the city plan—a grid pattern about one mile along the river and about one-half mile deep around an open square, or parade ground. Originally called Place d'Armes, this historic public area was renamed Jackson Square in 1851 to honor Andrew Jackson, hero of the Battle of New Orleans. The Vieux Carré, also known as the French Quarter, although only a small part of sprawling, twentieth-century New Orleans, is symbolic of the city; and Jackson Square is the heart from which its history and life radiate.

The Vieux Carré is a highly concentrated urban area of deep, narrow lots covering about 260 acres—some 105 blocks. The town was built on the natural levee, an elevation of about ten feet, but the river still flooded periodically. Residents soon learned to raise the principal floors of their dwellings, which were usually of cypress, above a one-story brick cellar. Terrible fires in 1788 and 1794 consumed almost the entire town, and, except for parts of the second Ursuline Convent, begun in 1748, no buildings remain from the French colonial period. The oldest surviving example of the prevalent early raised-cottage style is popularly known as Madame John's Legacy and was built in 1788 on Dumaine Street for Manuel Lanzos. Because of the fires, practically the whole French Quarter was rebuilt during Spanish colonial occupation. Remarkably, much of the French culture and style was retained, supplemented by certain notable Spanish contributions, such as the introduction of courtyards and wrought iron. In addition, new building codes required structures to be built of brick or a combination of brick and wood and covered with stucco or plaster. The most important building surviving from the Spanish era is the Cabildo, the city hall. It was designed as part of a pair of buildings flanking the St. Louis Cathedral on the Place d'Armes, but its twin, the Presbytère, on the downriver side of the cathedral, was not completed until much later, and both have since undergone significant alterations.

Although a few other late-eighteenth-century buildings survive from the Spanish period, most of the Vieux Carré today consists of rich, nineteenth-century antebellum construction, largely American, but greatly influenced by eighteenth-century French and Spanish traditions. Fundamentally, the special identity of the whole district represents the culture of colonial New France and New Spain as modified by the developing culture of young America.

In Creole fashion, structures in the Quarter are built directly at the street. Rear enclosed courtyards and service dependencies are found behind Creole cottages, two- and three-story stuccoed townhouses, frame shotgun houses (single and double), as well as behind the Anglo-American side-hall brick townhouses in the early American republic's favorite Federal and Greek Revival styles. These private, rear-garden living-spaces form the interior of each block, away from the street and *banquette* (sidewalk). Direct access to the life of the street is suggested by numerous French doors on the first and second floors, often onto balconies shading the *banquette*. Ornate cast iron was introduced in the 1820s and by 1850 was the height of fashion. Cast- and wrought-iron balconies eventually decorated many buildings in the city and have become symbolic of New Orleans in general and the French Quarter in particular. (A Creole balcony was usually a columnless, wrought-iron gallery; the Americans used heavier cast-iron supports.) The Creole convention of shops occupying the street-level floor of houses contributed to the rich texture of life in the Quarter.

There were, and are, commercial and industrial buildings, churches and related structures, markets, docks, warehouses, banks, restaurants, bars, groceries, shops, and governmental buildings throughout the Vieux Carré. This was for many years, after all, an entire city, and remained the center of local business activity until the 1830s.

By the twentieth century other areas of the city were more fashionable, but although it had become a bit run down, a great deal of the Quarter had survived with its aesthetic and historical integrity essentially intact. By 1920 the city began to rediscover its charm, and in 1925, to protect this picturesque and romantic colonial survivor from the "encroachment of modern business," the New Orleans city government created the Vieux Carré Association. Ambitious but ineffective, it was renamed the Vieux Carré Commission and strengthened in 1936 and 1937 by state and city laws that stipulated preservation regulations and officially delineated historic district boundaries.

The Vieux Carré was declared a National Historical Landmark District in 1965–66 and listed in the National Register of Historic Places. The *tout ensemble* within these boundaries is protected: an evolved environment made up of a combination of authentic elements, a sum total that contributes to its unique character and charm as a place to experience as well as live.

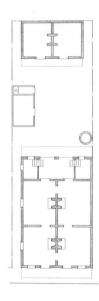

ABOVE LEFT: An American style townhouse and a Creole cottage, on Iberville Street between Dauphine and Burgundy; drawn by F. N. Tourne in 1859. [67.1] ABOVE RIGHT: Typical first-floor plan for a Creole cottage, with cabinets, *or storage rooms, at the rear separated by a loggia. Kitchen and privy are at the back of the courtyard. [67.2] (See pages 68–73.)*

ABOVE: Sindos-Latorre-Boucvalt house, c. 1841, St. Louis Street.[67.3] BELOW: Gauche-Gray-Stream house, 1856, Esplanade Avenue. [67.4]

DOLLIOLE-MASSON COTTAGE

1805; restored 1981, Frank Masson, architect
St. Philip Street, Vieux Carré

ABOVE: Front elevation. Built in 1805, this is a perfect archetypal Creole cottage. It was restored in 1981. BELOW: Front French door, looking through the dining room and kitchen to the rear courtyard. OPPOSITE: Front sitting room. Based upon important clues found in the building, doors, windows, and mantels were designed and re-created for the restoration.

THIS CLASSIC EXAMPLE of a Creole cottage was built by Jean-Louis Dolliole (1779–1861), a prominent free man of color in early nineteenth-century New Orleans. Creole cottages evolved from small urban houses in France and the French West Indies and became popular in the Vieux Carré and later Creole residential areas such as Faubourg Marigny. They were also built in the American Sector and may be found in the far uptown, even as far upriver as Carrollton. Typically, they were two rooms wide and two deep with

small *cabinets,* or storage rooms at the back corners of the house. They were built of brick, wood frame, or brick-between-posts.

Benjamin Henry Latrobe (1764–1820), the noted architect from Baltimore, visited New Orleans in 1819 and was intrigued by these one-story houses. He recorded his observations in detail: "The roofs are high, covered with tiles or shingles, and project five feet over the footway, which is also five feet wide. The eaves therefore discharge the water into the gutters. . . . However differ-

69   *Dolliole-Masson Cottage*

Looking from the rear chamber toward a front French door. The designs of the new kitchen, bathroom, bookcase, stair, and attic bedroom are all consistent with the style of the original cottage.

ent this mode is from the American manner of building, it has a very great advantage both with regard to the interior of the dwelling and to the street. . . . These one-storied houses are very simple in their plan. The two front rooms open into the street with French glass doors. . . . They do not require so much space for passages."

Louis Dolliole immigrated to New Orleans from France in the latter part of the Spanish period and became a prominent builder. Although Louisiana law prohibited miscegenetic marriages, Louis's rela-

tionship with Geneviève, a free woman of color, produced four offspring, considered free persons of color, whom he recognized as his children and heirs. Two of his sons, Jean-Louis and Joseph, followed in his footsteps to become builders and entrepreneurs, and had a significant influence in the development of Faubourg Tremé.

Free persons of color (*gens de couleur libres*) historically comprised an important segment of the New Orleans population; among them were talented craftsmen, musicians, and well-to-do tradesmen, many of

whom were property owners. Although their legal status in the French colony was defined in 1724 by the *Code Noir* (Black Code), the reality of being free and "of color" in a slaveholding colony and state caused predictable but not insurmountable problems. Within the larger context of the antebellum South, the achievements and stature of the free persons of color in New Orleans are remarkable.

Jean-Louis Dolliole built this house on land purchased from his father in 1804 and maintained a comfortable home for his family for

Rear chamber, looking into the courtyard garden. Plaster walls, historically correct color schemes, and longleaf pine floors complete the sense of authenticity.

many years. The inventory of his first wife's estate reveals many fine furnishings and accoutrements, and by the time the property was sold for $3,000 in 1854, Jean-Louis had amassed a respectable fortune.

When architect Frank Masson and his wife Ann purchased the house in 1980, the Dolliole house was a ruined shell abandoned for thirty years. The original kitchen building, cistern, and privy had been destroyed, but enough of the house remained to encourage this splendid restoration. The Massons have carefully restored and fur-

Rear elevation of the Massons' Creole cottage restoration. Private courtyards provide an almost year-round extension of the interior living space in the subtropical climate of New Orleans.

nished the house to recall the early 1800s; Masson designed hardware, mantels, and other architectural features in the style of the era when Dolliole built it, just after the Louisiana Purchase. French doors, shuttered for privacy, open onto the *banquette*, and there is a private rear courtyard where the family may gather to relax in the shade of a lovely cherry tree. Today, the Massons' home is one of the best surviving examples of those small Creole houses that Latrobe admired, and it is an important thread in the living fabric of the Vieux Carré.

Dolliole-Masson Cottage

WILLIAMS COTTAGE-DYKES GARDEN

Late eighteenth or early nineteenth century; exterior rebuilt 1916; restored 1980
Governor Nicholls Street, Vieux Carré

THE WILLIAMS COTTAGE, while somewhat different in exterior appearance from the Dolliole cottage, is still recognizable as being of the classic Creole type, which first appeared in Louisiana in the mid-eighteenth century and continued to be constructed into the twentieth century, by which time the type was spread throughout most of New Orleans. The interior of this charming frame duplex may predate the Dolliole cottage (possibly from the colonial period when twelve such cottages were sold in this block), but the exterior was rebuilt in the twentieth century. Nonetheless, it has all the earmarks of the practical story-and-a-half prototype, built at the *banquette* and raised slightly, with its deep eave sheltering guests and pedestrians.

The cottage had fallen into disrepair when Gary R. Williams, a leading Vieux Carré preservationist, acquired the property in 1972. He restored it for his home in 1980.

The rear of the lot was originally devoted to gardens and service buildings and is now a wonderfully lush, subtropical canvas for landscape contractor Rankin J. Dykes III, who shares residence of the duplex. The rear gallery of the cottage, which was a later addition, looks out on Dykes's creation, which has been featured in several books, including *The New American Garden, The Romantic Garden, Gardening With Style,* and *Garden Design.*

OPPOSITE: Front elevation. A Creole cottage, renovated by Gary R. Williams as a comfortable contemporary residence in the Vieux Carré. ABOVE: Rear elevation and garden. R. J. Dykes III is a landscape contractor, and the "cobbler's children," in this case the landscaper's garden, clearly did not suffer.

THIERRY-REAGAN HOUSE

1814, Latour & Latrobe, architects; restored 1940, Richard Koch, architect
Governor Nicholls Street, Vieux Carré

IN 1812 HENRY LATROBE (1792–1817), was sent to New Orleans to construct a grand waterworks plan conceived and designed by his father, the brilliant architect Benjamin Henry Latrobe (1764–1820). In 1814 young Latrobe collaborated with Arsène Lacarrière Latour, a French-born architect, on the design of this house for Jean Baptiste Thierry, editor of a New Orleans newspaper, *Le Courrier de la Louisiane.*

A sophisticated variation on the vernacular cottages built throughout the city, the Latrobe-Latour design was described in a contemporary account as an "elegant and convenient brick house, . . . consisting of five rooms, two *cabinets* and two cellars; with a kitchen likewise built of bricks, both terrace roofed and affording ample lodgings for servants; an extensive yard, and a flower garden

in front of the house."

Samuel Wilson, Jr., noted architect and architectural historian, was with Richard Koch's firm in 1940 and remembered that during the restoration for Miss Sarah Henderson, they discovered an open gallery that had been enclosed. They took the stucco off and could see the columns and arches. "The columns," he said, "were there with the moldings still intact where they closed them in." Wilson feels that Latrobe was responsible for the front, the Doric portico with segmental arches, while Latour probably designed the back, where a large arch is set between the two *cabinets* in the Creole French style.

Now that the Doric front of the cottage has been revealed and restored, it may be said to be the oldest Greek Revival house in the city, although there were earlier in-

stances of Greek details (e.g., the Doric portico on Latrobe's 1811 engine house for the waterworks). Roger G. Kennedy, in *Greek Revival America* wrote: "Henry Latrobe died young, but only after he had given the city its first Greek Revival building, in 1814."

Perhaps Latrobe's influence, too, is felt in the overall scheme, because the cottage is set back, instead of flush with the *banquette*, as was customary in the Vieux Carré. Consequently, there are front as well as rear patio gardens.

The present occupant, Thomas N. Reagan, is proud of his Greek Revival landmark, and maintains it in fine style. The rear garden, with a view of adjacent galleried service ells, has a particularly French Quarter ambience; within those walls it seems like the south of France, or Spain, transposed to Louisiana, in the true Creole tradition.

OPPOSITE: Front elevation. Richard Koch found Henry Latrobe's original Greek Revival gallery during the 1940 restoration; it is the oldest example extant in the city. TOP LEFT: Patio garden with service building to the left, containing the kitchen; beyond are neighboring service buildings with their characteristic angled roof lines. ABOVE LEFT: Rear elevation. Samuel Wilson, Koch's associate, believes this to be Latour's contribution to the Greek Revival cottage, reflecting the Creole building tradition in the great arch and flanking cabinets. ABOVE RIGHT: Entrance foyer with a view into the atrium, as restored in 1940.

Thierry-Reagan House

Magnon-Ingram-Stone House

1819, Gurlie & Guillot, architects-builders; restored 1968, Koch & Wilson, architects
Ursuline Street, Vieux Carré

ABOVE: *Front elevation on Ursuline Street. A Vieux Carré townhouse combining Greek Revival and Creole French influences.* BELOW: *Stair hall. The staircase was designed by Koch & Wilson in the 1968 restoration/renovation.*

AFTER THE FIRES of 1788 and 1794 razed much of the city in the area now called the French Quarter, new building codes were enacted. Consequently, this building, which originally had a first-floor storefront, was built of brick and had a terrace roof.

When this house was built the town was less than two decades removed from being a Spanish possession, and immigrants representing many diverse cultures were arriving daily, but New Orleans had retained a definite French flavor. The archi-

tects and builders were nearly all French, among them Barthélémy Lafon (1769–1820), Benjamin Buisson (1793–1874), and the architect-contractors Claude Gurlie and Joseph Guillot, who had added the second story to the Presbytère and built this house on Ursuline Street.

Koch & Wilson restored the house completely in 1968 for Frederick Ingram. It was a "million-dollar job," Wilson has said. The old chimneys were rebuilt with new flue linings and the appearance of the courtyard was changed considerably

ABOVE: Rear elevation with courtyard. BELOW: Loggia overlooking the garden courtyard. Koch & Wilson used this combination of French doors and fanlights in many of their historical designs in New Orleans.

with the addition of a guest wing and a swimming pool.

The building was originally two stories when Gurlie & Guillot designed and built it in 1819 for Arnaud Magnon, a shipbuilder who had a shipyard by the river at Ursuline Street. The city bought his shipyard to make a park for the citizenry, and Magnon used the proceeds to build this house. The top half-story addition was made about 1840 when the cupola was built and the style of the house was updated to Greek Revival, the favorite Neo-

classicism of young America. The house started out Creole French and ended American Neoclassical. (During Koch & Wilson's expensive, thoroughly researched restoration/renovation, Sam Wilson made a complete set of Historic American Buildings Survey drawings.)

Sam Wilson said that Fritz Ingram's idea was "to do the house better than it had been." Koch & Wilson's "plastic surgery" was eminently successful, and it is much appreciated by the present owner, James H. Stone.

Magnon-Ingram-Stone House

ABOVE: *The double parlors were decorated to complement the architecture and the French traditions of the Vieux Carré.*
OPPOSITE: *Dining room. The Robert Walker wall mural depicts New Orleans in the 1830s.*

Magnon-Ingram-Stone House

LE CARPENTIER-BEAUREGARD-KEYES HOUSE

1826, François Correjolles, architect
1113 Chartres Street, Vieux Carré

IN NEW ORLEANS, even in the Vieux Carré, the years from 1820 to 1835 witnessed a growing American influence in many aspects of business and social life. This was particularly evident in the architectural expression of the time as Anglo-American features, devices, and styles began to appear in conjunction with, and even in place of, the French, Spanish, and Creole patterns. One of the most important buildings of this transitional period, when the city was falling under the sway of the Americans, was the Joseph Le Carpentier house on Chartres Street, designed by architect François Correjolles, son of refugees from Santo Domingo. It was built by James Lambert, with modifications that made it part American and part French.

The center-hall plan and the pedimented portico of four Tuscan columns with exterior stairways extending from either side indicate the American Federal style. The front casement openings flanking the central doorway are French, however, and these "French doors," with delicate transoms protected by paneled shutters, continue the Creole tradition. The exterior walls are plastered and painted in the French and Spanish style, instead of the red Philadelphia brick being introduced locally at the time. Both the American and French colonials used the raised cottage format as appropriate to the hot and humid New World climate, so this aspect could point in either direction, but the placement of the house at the *banquette* is pure Vieux Carré. (Across the street is the convent of the Ursulines from whom Le Carpentier bought his large lot.)

Joseph Le Carpentier, a well-to-do auctioneer, was the maternal grandfather of Paul Charles Morphy, who is said to have been born in the house in 1837 and who later became one of the great chess masters of the world. Confederate General P. G. T. Beauregard (1818–1893), the "great Creole," rented here for eighteen months, 1866–1868, after the Civil War. Since that time, in his honor, it was almost always known as Beauregard House. In 1925, to save it from demolition, a group of New Orleans ladies and gentlemen raised funds and created Beauregard House, Inc., as a memorial to the gen-

Front elevation on Chartres Street. A New Orleans Federal period house that elegantly combines Creole French and Anglo-American influences. Open to the public.

Le Carpentier-Beauregard-Keyes House

ABOVE: Dining room overlooking courtyard. BELOW: Courtyard elevation. The Frances Parkinson Keyes Foundation restored the house under the guidance of Richard Koch of Koch & Wilson.

eral. In 1944 the novelist Frances Parkinson Keyes (1885–1970), leased a portion of it as her New Orleans headquarters and winter residence. Later the Keyes (rhymes with *wise*) Foundation acquired the entire property for restoration, which included the removal of an unsightly building where the reconstructed garden now stands. Richard Koch, and later Koch & Wilson, provided architectural consultation.

During her New Orleans sojourns Mrs. Keyes wrote *Madame Castel's Lodger*, about Beauregard and this house; *The Chess Players*, about Paul Morphy; and *Dinner at Antoine's*, about one of the city's classic restaurants. Mrs. Keyes left the house as a museum, which is open to the public. The Beauregard Chamber features heirlooms and memorabilia of the general and his family.

Parlors. The house museum recalls Confederate General P. G. T. Beauregard, who rented here for eighteen months from 1866 to 1868, and Mrs. Keyes, who maintained a seasonal residence here from 1944 until her death in 1970.

Le Carpentier-Beauregard-Keyes House

HERMANN-GRIMA HOUSE

1831–32, William Brand, architect-builder; Koch & Wilson, restoration architects
820 St. Louis Street, Vieux Carré

THIS IS A WELL-DOCUMENTED SITE that was opened to the public as a house museum in 1971. It was built for Samuel Hermann (1777–1853) by William Brand (1778–1849), a "master mason and contractor of buildings." Hermann, a native of Frankfort, Germany, was a well-to-do entrepreneur and commission merchant who came to New Orleans about 1813. William Brand was a native of Scotland who made his way to New Orleans by way of Virginia and Kentucky about 1805. Together these successful immigrants created a splendid brick three-story mansion on the south side of St. Louis Street.

Samuel Hermann and his family lived in an older home on the lot for about ten years before he commis-

Opposite top: Front elevation. A symmetrical, American late-Georgian façade at the banquette *of St. Louis Street. Open to the public. Opposite bottom: Rear elevation, with service wing and courtyard garden. Archaeological findings, family documentation, and extensive research helped authenticate garden details. Above: Parlor looking into dining room. The plan is Anglo-American and the furnishings, many of them American Empire, interpret New Orleans life during the rich antebellum period. The Colonial Dames of America assisted in furnishing the parlor.*

Hermann-Grima House

sioned Brand to create this house and compound in the format then becoming popular, a variation of American late-Georgian with Creole influences. The main house fronts directly on the street, with a rear service courtyard, garden, and servants' quarters-kitchen, which is in the typical Vieux Carré Creole style. The fanlight entrance, wide central hall, and tall, double-hung, sash windows are major Georgian elements, yet on the rear is a loggia flanked by Creole *cabinets*. There is no gallery shading the serenely symmetrical brick façade, painted red with white penciled mortar joints in the early American manner, but its wrought-iron balcony could not be more characteristic of this densely urban Creole neighborhood.

Judge Felix Grima (1798–1887), a New Orleans native and friend of Samuel Hermann, acquired the property in 1844 after Hermann suffered financial reversals. Judge Grima had nine children and his descendants lived here for several generations. They sold the property in 1921, and in 1924, the Christian Woman's Exchange (founded in 1881 to help needy women) took title and used the property to further the organization's charitable and educational goals. In 1971 the Women's Exchange opened the Hermann-Grima House and Courtyards on a permanent basis and listed it on the National Register of Historic Places. In 1974 the complex was designated a National Historic Landmark, and in 1986 it was accredited by the American Association of Museums. The house has been carefully restored and furnished appropriately with items from the 1830s to the 1860s. Some of the furnishings and decorative and fine arts belonged to the Felix Grima family and some are from the Hermanns.

Dining room with a view into the parlor. The Hermann and Grima families enjoyed affluent, even opulent, antebellum lifestyles, as reflected in the furnishings of the house museum.

Hermann-Grima House

ABOVE: Front elevation. One of the largest and finest private homes in the Vieux Carré, restored to the grandeur of its French Empire incarnation by Dr. Russell Albright. OPPOSITE: Entrance stair hall. Beyond the richly ornamented entrance vestibule, the central halls and winding stair access all levels of Trastour's design.

Lalaurie-Albright House
The "Haunted House"
1831; rebuilt 1837–38, Pierre Edouard Trastour, architect

THE LALAURIE-ALBRIGHT HOUSE is a compelling source of majesty and mystery—from its commanding presence one can appreciate the rich variety of the French Quarter, and through its fascinating history one can look back into a past checkered with outrageous cruelty and poignant compassion. The "Haunted House," as it became known, has undergone several striking structural and spiritual incarnations in its fabled existence.

The two-story house built in 1831 by Edmond Soniat Dufossat probably resembled the late-Georgian Hermann-Grima house on St. Louis Street more than it does the imposing edifice we see today. It was not quite finished when Dufossat sold it to Madame Delphine Macarty de Lopez Blanque Lalaurie, wife of the socially prominent Dr. Louis Lalaurie. According to contemporary newspaper accounts and later embellishments by author George Washington Cable in *Strange True Stories of Louisiana,* the tale of Madame Lalaurie's mansion is a classic of Southern gothic horror.

Behind the dignified façade on Royal Street, the Lalaurie slaves had been subjected to extraordinary privations and abuse until one, a cook, set fire to the house in a desperate attempt to attract attention to their awful plight. When neighbors saw the smoke and broke in, they discovered gruesome evidence of the Lalauries' insanity: under the same roof where they displayed expensive furniture and sophisticated art were hidden a half-dozen chained and manacled, starved and mutilated slaves. As word of the atrocities spread, an angry crowd of perhaps 2,000 gathered in the neighborhood, but Dr. and Madame Lalaurie apparently slipped away to a waiting ship and escaped to France. The outraged citizenry turned its fury on the house, looting and destroying its contents, leaving it a gutted ruin.

The house remained an empty reminder of its sor-

did past for several years, until it was purchased in 1837 by Pierre Edouard Trastour, architect and designer, who completely redesigned it, adding a third floor and transforming its style from conservative late-Georgian to elegant French Empire. Charles Caffin soon bought the unfinished project, completing construction in 1838 and overseeing the execution of Trastour's exuberant interior details.

The house and appurtenances changed ownership several times through the nineteenth century, serving primarily institutional uses until it evolved into Warrington House, a refuge for indigent men established by William J. Warrington. By the Great Depression, when Warrington House performed extraordinary humanitarian service to the community, the compound at Royal and Governor Nicholls seemed far removed from the bizarre events of a century before. The old stories of rattling chains and moaning ghosts of the Lalaurie slaves continued, however, and even today, the place is referred to on tours and in guidebooks as the "Haunted House."

These unquiet spirits did not inhibit Dr. Russell Albright, who took the house on as a restoration project in 1969. The architectural firm of Koch & Wilson advised and directed major renovations for him in 1976 and 1980. The interior design by Michael Myers, a resident of the house, complements Trastour's "spirited" 1837 work. Perhaps the ghosts, confused by alterations and renovations over the years—or placated by Mr. Warrington's noble kindness to indigent men—have finally fled (like Madame Lalaurie) to another venue. Unquestionably, the Lalaurie-Albright house deserves its place among classic New Orleans landmarks. It is a palace among the houses of the Vieux Carré, rising above them with cornice and cupola held high, despite the old whispers of its demon chatelaine.

RIGHT: *Parlors. A compendium of classical motifs line the ceiling friezes and cornices and decorate the doors of Trastour's interiors. Contemporary interior design is by Michael Myers.* BELOW: *Parlor door detail, mythological figures in delicate bas-relief.* ABOVE: *Dining room. The ornate plaster details and woodwork were executed by Caleb A. Parker in 1838.*

Lalaurie-Albright House

LOMBARD HOUSE

c. 1836
Bourbon Street, Vieux Carré

ABOVE: Front elevation. Greek Revival townhouse in the Vieux Carré, similar and perhaps related to the house at 1424 Royal Street.
BELOW LEFT: Rear elevation and courtyard garden, a typically private French Quarter sanctuary. BELOW RIGHT: Detail of rear garden.
OPPOSITE: Sitting room. The exotic interiors reflect the individuality and enthusiasm for life in the Vieux Carré.

BUILT FLUSH AGAINST THE *BANQUETTE,* with living spaces oriented toward an enclosed courtyard at the rear, the American Classical style townhouse continued the Creole urban tradition of residential privacy. Secure behind walls, shutters, jalousies, and closed doors, family life in the Vieux Carré has always been focused on the secluded interior patios and lush gardens.

This fine example of a typical stuccoed-brick townhouse in the Greek Revival style was probably built by Joseph Lombard, Sr., who owned the property from 1836 to 1842. There is very little documentation remaining that would fix exactly the building date and identify the architect, but certain theories can be extrapolated from related facts.

In 1826 Joseph Lombard built a Creole plantation manor house for his son, Joseph Lombard, Jr., in Faubourg McCarty. (The house, at 3933 Chartres, is still standing, the last survivor of this style.) Young Lombard died seven years later, and his widow, Azèle Zeringue Lombard, built a house in 1838 in Faubourg Marigny at 1424 Royal Street. The builders and designers of the

widow Lombard's Greek Revival townhouse were John Comminget and Peter McNulty, and they may have also designed this very similar house for her father-in-law on Bourbon Street.

An act of sale in 1886 described the Bourbon Street property as a "two-story, brick residence having on the ground floor, hall, sitting room, parlor, and dining room with sliding doors, pantry, and gallery in the rear; in the upper story, four bedrooms, dressing cabinet, open gallery in the rear with bath room and closet; a two-story brick building in the yard, having seven rooms, water works, privy, yard partly bricked and flagged, coach gate, etc. . . . ." The existing canopy and cast-iron balcony are later additions. To one side of the house is a carriage entrance leading to a large courtyard filled with subtropical vegetation.

The interiors were by George Segers of Dallas, Texas, described by the owner as a "peripatetic interior designer," who "decorated the large beautifully-proportioned rooms that open on a huge patio. The perfect note of humor is struck by majestic topiary. Did you expect to see an evergreen gorilla swinging from a tree in the Vieux Carré?"

Lombard House

DeSalvo House

"The Faulkner House"
1840
624 Pirate Alley, Vieux Carré

THE PAST-IN-THE-PRESENT that William Faulkner (1897–1962) perceived in the French Quarter clearly appealed to the young poet and aspiring author. For Faulkner the present was an extension of the past, a powerful legacy for the living, and through his later characters he declared that, in the South at least, the past was not even past. William Faulkner was a minor poet when he came to New Orleans in November 1924. At that time, the Vieux Carré undoubtedly formed an even more vivid *tout ensemble* of past and present than it does today. The aura of the Quarter left an indelible imprint on Faulkner's artistic imagination as he absorbed and transformed impressions while drinking large quantities of prohibition whiskey with the other writers and artists in the Paris (a Southern Paris) of America. Among those bohemians was Sherwood Anderson, an already published novelist, who thought the Creole and black ethnicity of New Orleans made it "the most civilized place" in America.

Anderson introduced Faulkner to William Spratling, who described how the two Williams first met: "When Bill Faulkner came to New Orleans he was a skinny little guy, three years older than I, and was not taken very seriously except by a few of us. I was living just back of the cathedral then [in an apartment in this house] with a heavy teaching schedule in architecture at Tulane. . . . A half-block away was Sherwood and Elizabeth Anderson in the Pontalba to one side of the cathedral front . . . . Sherwood said, 'Look, our friend Bill Spratling has an extra room there in Pirate's [*sic*] Alley. Why don't you just move over there with him?' So Faulkner did, and he was with me there, quietly and unobtrusively for many months."

Spratling remembered that when he woke up, Faulkner would already be "out on the little balcony tapping away on his portable," adding, "an invariable glass of alcohol-and-water at hand."

Spratling's description comes from a new edition of a rare little satirical volume of 400 copies he and Faulkner published in 1926 when they were apartment mates— *Sherwood Anderson and Other Famous Creoles*. Later, Spratling, a talented designer, became famous for founding the silver industry at Taxco, Mexico, and for his highly valued designs in silver—a major collection of his work is housed in the National Museum in Mexico City. Faulkner wrote his first novel, *Soldiers' Pay*, in this house in 1925. He needs no further introduction other than, perhaps, to remind the reader that in 1949 he was awarded the Nobel Prize for literature.

The building at 624 Pirate Alley, at the corner of Cabildo Alley, was built in 1840 by Marie Melasie Trepagnier LaBranche, the widow of Jean-Baptiste LaBranche, as one of a series of eleven brick, three- and four-story rowhouse-stores conceived for herself, members of her family, and other planter friends. All have multiple iron balconies, spiral staircases, and tiny courtyards linked by a little alley.

Today 624 Pirate Alley is the home of two busy professional people, Rosemary James and her husband, Joseph J. DeSalvo, Jr., who purchased the house in December 1988 and are completing a lengthy renovation. DeSalvo, an attorney, has a rare book store, Faulkner House Books, in a portion of the ground floor, which is the headquarters of the Pirate Alley Faulkner Society. Ms. James is responsible for the renovation and interior decoration of their Pirate Alley home, aided by a host of New Orleans artisans and specialists. This energetic, creative couple continues the tradition that Faulkner loved about the Vieux Carré—the past here really is not *past.*

ABOVE: The Faulkner House is at 624 Pirate Alley, across from St. Anthony's Garden at the rear of the St. Louis Cathedral.
OPPOSITE: Detail of library. Silver tea service by William Spratling.

DeSalvo House

DUREAU STUDIO AND RESIDENCE
c. 1840; renovated c. 1870
Dauphine Street, Vieux Carré

TOP: Front elevation. Dureau's balcony-gallery-garden off of his living room. RIGHT: Dureau's residence and art gallery, displaying some of his canvases. BELOW: Detail of the artist's studio-residence, with views of the Vieux Carré.

ON THE SECOND FLOOR of this large, mid-nineteenth-century Creole building near the Esplanade edge of the French Quarter, artist George Dureau keeps a studio and residence, thereby continuing the urban tradition of the Vieux Carré, where buildings often were designed with commercial space on the ground floor with dwellings above. This brick, Classical Revival building was undoubtedly designed as such, and was probably built about 1840 for rental property by Noël Barthélémy

Le Breton and his wife, Henriette Ganucheau.

The property went through a series of owners in the nineteenth century, and for years housed a furniture company, before it was gutted long ago for warehouse space. Dureau moved into the loft-like upper floor during the 1970s and continues to make renovations at his own casual, artist's pace, when the "daemon" moves him. Located at the corner of Dauphine and Barracks streets, Dureau's home-studio-gallery overlooks a small green

park and playground, making his balcony, which spills over with huge plants, a pleasant and relaxing place to observe the life of his neighborhood.

This mixed-use location was part of the first Vieux Carré Historic Preservation Area. Established in 1925 by city ordinance, it consisted of twenty-two full squares and parts of many more. The area was increased in 1936 to 100 squares, and the Vieux Carré Commission was established the next year. The Vieux Carré Ordinance was amended several times but still consists largely of regulations that existed as of 1941.

At the turn of the century, when much of the Quarter had become a bit run down, before the "establishment" recognized its intrinsic value, artists and writers found it to be a congenial environment for the growth and free expression of their genius. Today, as evidenced by George Dureau and others in the community, the Vieux Carré is still a source of comfort, sustenance, and inspiration for artists.

Dureau Studio and Residence

THE 1850 HOUSE, LOWER PONTALBA BUILDING

1850–51, James Gallier, Sr., and Henry Howard, architects; Koch & Wilson, Henry Krotzer, Jr., restoration architects
523 St. Ann Street, Vieux Carré

The Pontalba buildings frame Jackson Square, the heart of New Orleans. This view over the top of the Upper Pontalba Building shows the St. Louis Cathedral to the left. Adjacent is the Presbytère and the red-brick Lower Pontalba Building. In the center of the square is the monument to Andrew Jackson, designed by Clark Mills.

THE LONG, RED-BRICK PONTALBA BUILDINGS face each other across Jackson Square just as they have since 1850–51. Their continuing existence is a story of preservation success, but the tale of their conception is more fascinating—a story of iron will and entrepreneurial brilliance.

Baroness Micaëla Almonester de Pontalba inherited the land flanking the old Place d'Armes from her father, Don Andrés Almonester y Roxas, a wealthy Spaniard who had rebuilt the Cabildo, Presbytère, and St. Louis Cathedral after the fire of 1788. The baroness, who was living in France, recognized that competition from the booming American Sector in 1840s New Orleans was depressing the value of her commercial property, so she developed a master plan to rekindle interest in the area. The crucial element was truly inspired—she persuaded the city authorities to Americanize the name of the public area to Jackson Square, honoring Andrew Jackson, the hero of the Battle of New Orleans.

Her design, drawn in France, was comprehensive; the entire development, incorporating the handsome cathedral, Cabildo, and Presbytère, would resemble a great public square, such as the Palais Royal or Place de Voges in Paris. The resulting composition is still one of the most aesthetically successful public areas in the United States, but in 1850 it was the set piece for her real estate venture. Her twin rows of townhouses frame the square, and although the names of two famous New Orleans architects are associated with their design, and one of the city's leading contractors was involved in their construction, the imperious baroness practically designed and built them herself. She determined what she wanted and would not be deterred—she considered *herself* to be the architect and contractor.

Parlor. Much of the furniture on exhibit in the rooms upstairs came from the Fernando Puig home, 624 Royal Street, a house in that family's possession for over a century. Many fine pieces on exhibit are attributed to one of the city's most famous cabinetmakers and furniture dealers, Prudent Mallard, a native Frenchman who immigrated to New Orleans early in the nineteenth century.

When completed, each row contained sixteen separate houses on the upper floors and self-contained shops at square level. The cast-iron galleries, probably the city's first of this type, were in Gallier's original design. They shade the *banquette* and provide balconies for the apartments. Railings decorated with heart-shaped cartouches bearing the monogram "AP" signify the Almonester and Pontalba families. Building materials for the project came through the port from the Atlantic states and abroad: granite from New England, pressed brick from Baltimore, plate glass, slate, and roofing tiles from England, window glass from New Jersey, and ornamental iron from New York.

After the Civil War the neighborhood had declined, especially after the baroness's death in 1874, and by the turn of the century, the Pontalba buildings had become tenements. In 1921 William Ratcliffe Irby, a New Or-

leans philanthropist who was a pioneer in preserving historic landmarks in the French Quarter, bought the Lower Pontalba Building from the Pontalba heirs and willed it to the Louisiana State Museum, which came into possession of it in 1927. Later, the City of New Orleans acquired the Upper Pontalba Building.

During the 1930s the Work Projects Administration funded an extensive renovation on both buildings and subdivided the townhouses into apartments, but restoration work on the Lower Pontalba Building is an ongoing project. In 1955, 523 St. Ann Street was restored, and the rooms of the second and third floors were furnished as examples of a fine New Orleans townhouse of the 1850s. The first floor, which was originally a hardware store, now houses the museum gift shop and has some displays of items donated by Pontalba descendants.

1850 House, Lower Pontalba Building

GALLIER HOUSE MUSEUM
1857–58, James Gallier, Jr., architect
1132 Royal Street, Vieux Carré

IN 1857 ARCHITECT James Gallier, Jr. (1827–1868), designed this elegant Vieux Carré townhouse as his residence. The building reflects the young architect's eclectic and stylish taste, as well as his innovative ideas about residential comfort. A cast-iron cooking range, a complete plumbing system with an indoor bathroom, and passive ventilation are some of the progressive features Gallier incorporated in his home.

Gallier's father, James Gallier, Sr. (1798–1866), an Irish-born architect who specialized in Greek Revival de-signs, had immigrated to New York from London with his family in 1832, found work with James Dakin and then Minard Lafever, and eventually moved to New Orleans in 1834. For the following fifteen years, his name was associated with the design and construction of many outstanding New Orleans land-marks, such as the St. Charles Hotel (1835–38), the Second Municipality Hall (designed 1844, dedicated 1853, now called Gallier Hall), and the Pontalba Buildings (preliminary design, 1849). Failing eyesight

OPPOSITE TOP: Entrance façade. The brick house is covered with stucco, shaped and painted to imitate granite blocks on the first floor and smooth stone blocks elsewhere. The side-hall entrance is to the left, with a gate for the porte-cochère *on the right. OPPOSITE: Rear courtyard. ABOVE: Upstairs stair hall. Gallier used the upstairs hall with its skylight and gasolier as a library. The furnishings reflect items listed in the 1868 inventory. FOLLOWING PAGES: Double parlors shown as they would have appeared during the intense heat of New Orleans summers. Gallier House is one of the few house museums to exhibit this aspect of mid-nineteenth-century interior design.*

Gallier House Museum

caused him to retire from active practice in 1849, when he turned his office over to his talented son. Born in England and educated in America, James Gallier, Jr., designed many commercial buildings and fine dwellings, but perhaps his most distinctive commissions were the French Opera House (1859), the Florence A. Luling house (1865), and the Bank of America (1865), one of two structural cast-iron building fronts surviving in the city. The two Galliers had a profound influence on the architectural development of New Orleans at the height of its nineteenth-century economic energy.

In 1866 James Gallier, Sr., died in a steamship accident, and only two years later, James, Jr., still a young man at forty-one, passed away at home. The house remained in the family until 1917 but soon after fell into disrepair. After many years of neglect, restoration work was undertaken by the Ella West Freeman Foundation. Guided by Gallier's own drawings, architect Henry W. Krotzer, Jr., of Koch & Wilson, Architects, supervised the meticulous restoration, and the Gallier House Museum opened in 1971. The interiors were designed by Samuel Dornsife, and Dr. Jessie Poesch of Tulane University served as furniture consultant. Work continues today, dictated by ongoing research and the unrelenting subtropical climate. Frank W. Masson, A.I.A., supervised recent repairs and restorations.

A tour of the Gallier House Museum is a delightful trip back in time to the mid-nineteenth century. The house was built of brick and covered with stucco, which was shaped and painted to imitate granite on the downstairs front, and scored and painted to resemble large blocks of stone on the other walls. A rose-patterned, Paris-green, cast-iron veranda adorns the street façade and shades the lower walls and *banquette* from the summer sun. The rear courtyard was completely restored, as were appurtenant structures.

Careful archaeological investigation of the interior surfaces revealed hidden paint colors, marbling, and woodgraining, enabling craftsmen to simulate their original appearance. Gasoliers, mantels, and other surviving details were refurbished and returned to their proper locations. A detailed inventory taken at the time of James Gallier, Jr.'s, death in 1868 served as the basis for furnishing the home with approximately 6,000 period objects that reflect the domestic life of a prosperous family in the 1860s.

The Gallier house is designated a National Historic Landmark and was one of the first house museums accredited by the American Association of Museums. In 1986 Gallier's home and two 1832 auxiliary buildings were donated to Tulane University. The house and grounds are open to the public for tours, programs, and workshops for adults and children.

Gallier House Museum

ABOVE: A street scene in Faubourg St. Mary in 1821. [104.1]
BELOW: Canal Street, c. 1858, photograph by Jay Dearborn Edwards; Christ Church is on the right. [104.2]

Central Business District

The first suburb developed outside the original city plan was the Faubourg Ste. Marie (Faubourg St. Mary), which was subdivided from the old Bienville Plantation immediately upriver from the Vieux Carré by the Gravier family in 1788. At first it grew slowly and building remained close to the river, but after the Louisiana Purchase Americans began to settle the area, and by the 1820s it was beginning to grow and prosper. By the 1830s it was replacing the Vieux Carré as the business center of the city. Much of the American Sector, as the area became known, is now designated the Central Business District, which extends from Canal Street to Howard Avenue and from the river to Loyola Avenue. Within the Central Business District are four locally designated districts: Canal Street, Lafayette Square, Warehouse, and Picayune Place.

Several years after the Louisiana Purchase the city fortifications were removed and the commons area between the old city and the Faubourg St. Mary was retained for a public thoroughfare and a canal. The street was named Canal, and, although the canal itself was never built, the area reserved for its construction became an unusually wide median, dubbed the "neutral ground" between the American and French communities; today medians throughout the city are known as such. The location and distinctive proportions of Canal Street quickly attracted developers. By 1850 it had become the retail merchandising heart of the city, but prior to the Civil War, residences

Canal Street between Carondelet and Baronne streets, by Marie Adrien Persac, c. 1873. The fifth building from the right is now the Boston Club, a house originally built for Dr. William Newton Mercer in 1844. [104.3]

The Business District from St. Patrick's Church in 1852. Lafayette Square and Gallier Hall are to the left. [105.1]

and businesses were mixed along both sides of the street. Some houses were still being built in the 1860s and 1870s up Canal away from the river, but commerce eventually triumphed over residential, and only a single major residence remains: built in 1844 for William Newton Mercer and designed by James Gallier, Sr., it is located at 824 Canal Street and is now the Boston Club.

By the 1850s retail activity was taking over with the construction of stores and office buildings, often embellished with cast-iron balconies which protected pedestrians on the sidewalks below from the extremes of the subtropical climate. Many of these distinctively New Orleans balconies lasted into the twentieth century. A few ornate cast-iron façades were erected, but only one of these still stands, at 622 Canal. Built in 1857, it was designed by William A. Freret. Substantial office buildings began to replace the smaller storefronts in the second half of the century, and, in the early 1900s, high-rise structures like the Maison Blanche and Audubon buildings devoured even more. Large-scale hotel construction, as well as a decline in the number of retail stores continues to alter Canal Street, once one of the busiest urban promenades in America. The Canal Street Historic District was created in 1984.

The section of the Central Business District surrounding Lafayette Square, and now known as the Lafayette Square Historic District, was a fashionable residential section of the American Sector in the decades after the Louisiana Purchase. The street plan dates from 1788 and includes the public park, originally Place Gravier (for the family that developed the faubourg) but renamed in honor of the Marquis de Lafayette in 1824.

The best known building in the district is Gallier Hall, 545 St. Charles Avenue, facing Lafayette Square. This fine Greek Revival building, designed by James Gallier, Sr., and erected between 1845 and 1853, served as

Lafayette Square in 1858 was the center of an elegant residential neighborhood. St. Patrick's (left) and the First Presbyterian (right) churches are in the background. [105.2]

Neighborhoods Gazetteer

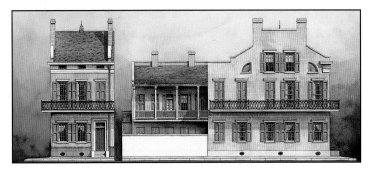

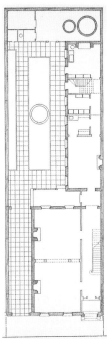

Townhouses were built in the French Quarter and nearby suburbs from the mid-eighteenth to the mid-nineteenth century. They were generally built to the sidewalk, shared party walls with adjacent buildings, and had a courtyard in the rear. Usually two or three stories, they had service rooms in a rear building or wing. The Creole townhouse typically had a shop on the ground floor and living quarters above, with entry to the residence through a side passageway from the street. The American townhouse was introduced about 1830 and was usually of red brick with white trim, with the main rooms on the ground floor, although Creole influences were often apparent. The house illustrated above was built on Camp Street in Faubourg St. Mary. [106.1 and 2]

Preservation Resource Center, 604 Julia Street, Julia Row. [106.3]

the New Orleans City Hall until 1957. Even today, the square is a center of government buildings, including the old Post Office (1915) and Federal Reserve Bank (1964). Another prominent structure is St. Patrick's Roman Catholic Church, 724 Camp Street. Begun in 1838, the Gothic Revival design is the work of Charles and James Dakin with construction supervision by James Gallier, Sr., who simplified the Dakins' design and completed the building in 1841. For many years this towering landmark was the highest building in New Orleans.

In the 1830s developers and architects brought an eastern seaboard building type to New Orleans—the row townhouse. The quality of the Greek Revival style of these red-brick, white-trimmed rows was exceptional, and the most notable surviving example is Julia Row, the thirteen townhouses that form the upriver side of the 600 block of Julia Street. Begun in 1832 and completed the following year, the row was probably designed by Alexander T. Wood for the New Orleans Building Company. Julia Row was once the best address in the city and later, one of the worst—until 1976 when the Preservation Resource Center restored and moved its headquarters into number 604.

The years after the Civil War saw a change in the area, as commercial activities began to dominate toward the first years of our century. Residences were demolished and replaced with business buildings and eventually with service stations and parking lots. The historic character of the area was in danger of disappearing completely before being recognized as intrinsically valuable. It is presently the center of successful historic preservation activities, driven by a force of spirited people willing to invest in homes, offices, shops, and other businesses, excited to live and work here again. A great deal of credit for this new spirit of neighborhood renovation is due to the Lafayette Square Association and the Historic Faubourg St. Mary Corporation.

Until 1805 the river levee was as far inland as Tchoupitoulas Street. The *batture*—the land between the levee and the river—was slowly reclaimed and developed, and in the 1840s long city blocks paralleling the river were established for huge warehouses. Several from the 1850s still survive within a few blocks of the massive new Convention Center. This area between the Lafayette Square District and the Convention Center is now called the Warehouse District. It has been devoted to various commercial functions of the port, wholesale and retail, since the early 1800s, but, unlike its Lafayette neighbor, which changed from residential to commercial, the warehouses are now being converted to homes.

An elegantly detailed four-story Greek Revival style warehouse at 448 Julia Street, from the 1830s, represents the basic warehouse type that would predominate for many years. There were rows of these, some with cast-iron ground floor columns, but many were demolished in the early twentieth century to make way for larger structures built to accommodate heavier manufacturing. The Gulf Bag Company, built in 1906 at 329 Julia Street, was among the first of that type. This and similar buildings have been converted with great style to upscale apartments, shops, restaurants, and art galleries. The district has been the center of considerable redevelopment—residential and commercial—since the late 1970s and especially since the Louisiana World Exposition in 1984.

Appropriately, the Picayune Place Historic District is small, but it is not trivial, as it contains a major concentration of nineteenth-century commercial buildings of architectural and historical significance. Its name is derived from the block-long street behind a fine row of buildings known as Newspaper Row, which once housed most of the city's newspapers, including the *Daily Picayune*. This district contains a dense urban environment with minimal open space. There has been little overall change in the district since World War I, and a visit here is a step back in time to an earlier and less hectic business world.

BELOW: Newspaper Row in the late 1880s. [107.1] TOP RIGHT: Julia Street redevelopment. At left center is Gallery Row, a residential and commercial redevelopment including a 1912 building and a c. 1830 red-brick row of stores. [107.2] RIGHT: Magazine Place apartments were converted from the 1910 Swift Foods Wholesale Market building. [107.3] LOWER RIGHT: Julia Place apartments were adapted from a turn-of-the-century warehouse. [107.4]

Neighborhoods Gazetteer

GREEN-PETERS-CAMPBELL HOUSE
1832; renovated 1987, Barron and Toups, architects
Julia Street, Central Business District

THIS AWARD-WINNING RENOVATION is one of the oldest houses remaining from the Faubourg St. Mary. The area was a desirable residential neighborhood in the decades after the Louisiana Purchase, when developers such as Samuel J. Peters (1801–1855) set out to create a modern New Orleans outside of the boundaries and conventions of the old Vieux Carré. Peters, who owned much of the property in the rapidly developing faubourg, bought an unfinished row of three, three-story masonry houses from fellow developer John Green in 1832, the same year the nearby and notable Julia Row (the Thirteen Sisters) was being erected. The Americanization of New Orleans was becoming evident in the construction of brick-front row houses such as these fine examples, but their style was not universally

admired. As early as 1819, Benjamin Latrobe, who obviously favored the eclectic charm of the Vieux Carré, had complained that "the red brick fronts are . . . gaining ground, & the suburb St. Mary, the American suburb, already exhibits the flat, dull, dingy character of Market Street in Philadelphia, . . . instead of the motley & picturesque effect of the stuccoed French buildings of the city. We shall introduce many grand & profitable improvements, but they will take the place of much elegance, ease, & some convenience."

Many buildings from this era were designed with a combination of features from several styles, according to the preferences and needs of the clients. The exterior of this group of houses is in the restrained Anglo-American Federal style, whereas the interior plan reflects the local

OPPOSITE: Front elevation as renovated in 1987. A shop below and residence above in the pattern of old New Orleans.
ABOVE: Sitting room. Campbell makes this his home, contributing to the neighborhood revitalization by living and working his ideals. He
and his partners received an award for Best Renovation of 1987 from the New Orleans Historic District Landmarks Commission.

Creole pattern of living, focusing on an interior court-yard. (The inclusion of a courtyard was frequently adapted by American designers and builders because it was so well suited to the climate.)

Adaptation is a key word for this house, for it was renovated in 1987 into a building that functions in a way typical of this city, wherein the upstairs is residential, and the ground floor commercial. Presently one of the numerous art galleries that characterize the renovated neighborhood occupies the street floor, which is appropriately entered through one of the ubiquitous French doors of the city.

David Campbell, who resides in one of the three houses, had two partners in the row renovation, John C. Abajian and the late Patrick J. Quinlivan. Campbell, a

leading preservationist who has been president of the Preservation Resource Center, is an attorney practicing out of an office in the former LaBelle Creole Cigar and Tobacco Factory (1882) at 755 Magazine Street. That Campbell has his residence and office in this part of the Central Business District reveals a dramatic change of direction for the area, and a reversion to earlier patterns that formerly characterized the American Sector. Once again genteel residential life and gentlemanly business and professional pursuits are closely juxtaposed. A champion of the Lafayette Square Historic District, David L. Campbell perhaps reincarnates the spirit of its old "mayor," Samuel J. Peters, in a house that Peters owned only a few years after the Marquis de Lafayette visited New Orleans.

Faubourg Marigny, c. 1821. [110.1]

ABOVE: Marigny plantation house, late-eighteenth century, detail from a map by Vinache. The view of New Orleans in 1803 by John L. Boqueta de Woiserie [28.1], is said to have been from this porch. [110.2] OPPOSITE TOP: Esplanade Avenue, Faubourg Marigny, 1834, by John H. B. Latrobe. [111.1] OPPOSITE CENTER: Esplanade Avenue at Royal Street, c. 1858, by Jay Dearborn Edwards. [111.2] OPPOSITE BOTTOM: The restored Henrietta Hudson shotgun cottage on Burgundy Street was built about 1890 and is typical of the nineteenth-century residential charm of the district. [111.3]

Faubourg Marigny District

In 1806, as the American Sector was developing with increasing momentum, Faubourg Marigny, the first Creole suburb, was laid out on the downriver side of the Vieux Carré. The colorful Bernard Xavier Philippe de Marigny de Mandeville (1775–1868), a New Orleans native whose first wife was an American, subdivided the large plantation he had inherited from his father. The plantation had originally belonged to Claude Joseph Villars Dubreuil, a wealthy planter and contractor and one of the most important figures in French Colonial New Orleans.

A French engineer, Nicolas de Finiels, planned the division of the property into lots and streets, and de Marigny gave them interesting names like Bagatelle and Craps, a clue to his fondness for games of chance. The plan, though skillfully conceived to one day join the streets of its neighboring predecessor, was also devised to conform to the extreme bend of the river and resulted in some odd bits of geometry, like the wedge formed between Esplanade and Elysian Fields now called the Marigny Triangle. Barthélémy Lafon, a city surveyor who also laid out the upriver area now known as the Lower Garden District, executed de Finiels's plan over the course of several years.

De Marigny found willing buyers and his suburb developed rapidly, encouraging the extension of the original layout a few blocks further inland from the river. The early residents of Faubourg Marigny were French and Spanish Creoles and a considerable number of free persons of color, many of whom had been employed as artisans in the various enterprises of the estimable Monsieur Dubreuil. Later years saw an influx of Irish, Italian, and German immigrants. The latter settled in such concentration that their neighborhood became known as Little Saxony.

Unlike the Vieux Carré or Faubourg St. Mary, Marigny has been primarily residential, although in the nineteenth century there were some large brick business buildings and cotton warehouses. The population of the faubourg was, for the most part, working class, and a majority of early houses were of the type we now call the Creole cottage. Single and double shotgun cottages trimmed in various Victorian styles began to be built in the 1840s and continued in popularity into the twentieth century. Except for Washington Square, which was part of de Marigny's original layout, there is little streetside foliage, as most of the houses were built close to the *banquette*; but behind the cottages was a private green world of subtropical gardens, much as in the adjacent French Quarter.

The character of the faubourg today remains nineteenth-century—a small-scaled, urban, yet intimate, neighborhood—architecturally and ethnically diverse. There are dominating church spires, rising above the Creole cottages and shotguns, corner shops, bars, and groceries, and here and there is a raised center-hall villa or a free-standing three-bay townhouse. There are remnants of a Greek Revival structure known as Architects Row and of cotton warehouses in the Press Street vicinity.

In the early 1970s preservationists began to move into the neighborhood, and, led by Dr. Eugene Cizek, an architectural professor and resident, they formed the Faubourg Marigny Improvement Association. Working with the City Planning Department, Cizek's Tulane University architecture students developed a comprehensive zoning recommendation that was adopted by the city. New zoning ordinances helped encourage even more of a neighborhood revival in this initial Creole suburb.

Neighborhoods Gazetteer

DOLLIOLE-DAVIS COTTAGE
1820; renovated 1960s, Arthur Q. Davis, architect
Bourbon Street, Faubourg Marigny District

Entrance façade on Bourbon Street.

THIS QUAINT BUT UNUSUAL five-sided Creole cottage was built to conform to the wedge-shaped lot created where the street pattern in the Faubourg Marigny merged into the Vieux Carré. These odd-shaped lots were not unusual in the faubourgs outside of the original town grid, because designers and engineers had to adjust their street schemes to accommodate the winding curves of the river and the patterns of adjacent existing neighborhoods. This lot is located where Rue Bagatelle (now Pauger Street) angled into Rue Bourbon.

Jean-Louis Dolliole, the builder whose own cottage is the now restored Dolliole-Masson cottage on St. Philip Street, built this interesting design solution in 1820 on a lot he purchased from his mother-in-law, Catherine Dusuau. Dolliole was an important business and social leader in the community of *gens de couleur libres* (free

persons of color), and he constructed a number of homes in the Creole sections of the city.

This stuccoed brick-between-posts cottage still has the original French pantile roof. The technique of using flat tiles tongued to lap over wooden boards without the use of nails is common in France and was once prevalent in New Orleans. The upturned pitch of the roof at its eaves is a style borrowed from earlier Louisiana colonial architecture. The unusual house was renovated in the mid-twentieth century by architect, artist, scholar, and writer, Lewis Clapp, who cut down the series of French doors opening onto the *banquette* to double-hung windows.

In the late 1960s Mr. and Mrs. Arthur Q. Davis purchased the cottage and began the renovations evident today, including the significant modifications Mrs.

ABOVE: Living room looking toward the rear addition. BELOW: Rear elevation and addition. Arthur Davis designed the addition to harmonize with the original cottage, which, although modified front and rear by the previous owner, still had many of its early features in place.

Davis made to the grounds and gardens. Arthur Q. Davis is a well-known architect, a graduate of Tulane and Harvard, who worked for a time with Eero Saarinen before starting his own firm in 1947 in New Orleans. His firm still does a few houses each year in addition to very large projects such as the Superdome. He believes: "Regional architecture should include historical elements and a respect for the climate, the terrain, and the surroundings."

In renovating this Marigny cottage for his home, Davis designed a rear addition to complement and harmonize with the original building; he used old handmade bricks and antebellum weathered cypress. He commented: "Much of the original hand-wrought, iron hardware is still in use. The hand-cut, beaded ceiling beams and battered shutters are also original [materials]."

Dolliole-Davis Cottage

ABOVE AND OPPOSITE TOP: Built at the banquette, *Sun Oak is a triple cottage with a service way between two units. A rusticated wood façade is covered by a gallery with slender Doric box columns. The vivid paint colors are part of Cizek's 1970s restoration. OPPOSITE BOTTOM: Parlor entrance. The Creole cottage is furnished throughout to suit the period, c. 1840. Wallpaper borders and appropriate window hangings set the stage for important collections of antique Louisiana furniture.*

NATHAN-LEWIS-CIZEK HOUSE

c. 1806; rebuilt and remodeled 1836;
restored 1976–79, Eugene Cizek, architect
Burgundy Street, Faubourg Marigny

IN THIS RARE AND TRULY UNIQUE tripartite Greek Revival galleried Creole cottage resides important leadership in the revitalization of the Faubourg Marigny Historic District—Eugene Cizek, restoration architect and professor, and Lloyd Sensat, Jr., artist and teacher. Practically the "community house" for the Faubourg Marigny Improvement Association, and in fact open to the public by appointment as an art gallery and inn, Sun Oak cottage was restored by Cizek with Sensat's help between 1976 and 1979. In the renovation the triplex was reduced to a duplex, combining two units as one apartment. Christopher Friedrichs, a preservation-minded landscape archi-

ABOVE: *Looking from the parlor toward a bedroom and spiral staircase beyond. The portrait of Asher Nathan and his son, Achille, was painted by Jules Lion, a free man of color and a noted nineteenth-century artist.* OPPOSITE: *These back-to-back staircases are now part of one unit, a combination of two apartments originally separate. The resident ghost, a small old lady dressed in black is said to use this staircase occasionally, that is, Cizek says, when she is not busy "moving furniture."*

tect, assisted them with the grounds, especially the tropical gardens surrounding a large oak tree shading the rear patios and courtyards. Providing advice for the authentically interpreted interiors was H. Parrott Bacot, a Louisiana museum and history expert.

Cizek and Sensat have set lively and exceptional standards for the renovation and general improvement of their immediate community. Both men have received considerable recognition for their innovative teaching, co-authoring and implementing the award-winning programs "Education Through Historic Preservation" and "Quarter Kids: Learning from the Vieux Carré."

One cannot miss Sun Oak, built at the *banquette*, with its long, rusticated façade unifying three apartments and a dogtrot, and painted a Creole color scheme of French Red, Putty, Indigo, and Egyptian Blue. Five rooms deep, the cottage triplex has Greek Revival interiors with medallions, moldings, mantels, and millwork in that antebellum style, popular even in this Creole faubourg. Highlighted underfoot by deep red mahogany-colored pine floors, all rooms are furnished with choice examples of French, Creole, Acadian and Mid-French

Louisiana antiques. Delicate winding staircases lead to the dormered bedrooms.

The Faubourg Marigny was laid out in 1806 just downriver from the Vieux Carré for plantation owner and developer Bernard de Marigny, a native Creole, who named this street Rue Craps for his love of the dice game. It is now somewhat more blandly called Burgundy Street. In 1806 Constance Rixner Bouligny, a free woman of color, purchased this lot and erected a brick-between-posts cottage, but by 1836, when Asher Moses Nathan bought the house, it was in deplorable condition. Nathan, a Jewish immigrant from Amsterdam, remodeled the house using portions of the original structure and transforming its style to Greek Revival.

In 1843 the house was sold to Algernon Sidney Lewis, son of Judge Joshua Lewis, who had been appointed district court judge after the Louisiana Purchase. By 1850 it had been sold again for rental use and began its gradual decline toward slum status. Today, thanks to the commitment and efforts of Cizek and Sensat, Sun Oak is a model and inspiration for historic preservation in New Orleans

Nathan-Lewis-Cizek House

ABOVE: *New Orleans author Grace King (1851–1932) lived in this Greek Revival house overlooking Coliseum Square from 1904 until her death. The present owners are descendants of Miss King. The house was built in 1849 for Frederick Rodewald. [118.1]*
BELOW: *St. Anna's Asylum, built in 1857 on Prytania Street, has been restored and is an important landmark in the classical context of the Lower Garden District. [118.2]*

Lower Garden District

In 1806 Barthélémy Lafon (1769–1820), the architect and parish surveyor who was laying out Faubourg Marigny according to de Finiels's plan, was commissioned to subdivide the Delord-Sarpy Plantation just above (upriver from) Faubourg St. Mary. Lafon ultimately created a grand master plan that included several plantations. He designed the layout to conform to the fan-shaped boundaries of the plantations being developed and to follow the bend in the river, so that streets paralleling the river roughly echo its curve, like ripples from its levee. Cross streets running away from the river form a general radial pattern inward, like the pleats of an accordion when squeezed at the top. This solution resulted in some oddly angled intersections and irregularly shaped lots, but it enabled the plan to follow the relatively high ground along the river and was used in similar fashion in other faubourgs.

Compared to the apparent whimsy with which de Marigny had named the streets in his downriver development—Craps, Good Children, Prosper, and Josephine, for example—Lafon's plan seems almost grandiloquent. Streets were given classical names, like those of the nine Greek Muses: Calliope, Clio, Erato, Thalia, Melpomene, Terpsichore, Euterpe, Polymnia, and Urania. Prytania, a main street through Lafon's conception, refers to a prytaneum, a great public building he had planned. Much of the elaborate plan for the early Greek Revival faubourg was only partly implemented: a circular park, the Place du Tivoli, is now Lee Circle; a long park that was to be dominated by a huge coliseum is Coliseum Square; and the large Place de l' Annonciation was intended as the site of a cathedral. Ultimately, the subdivision of adjacent upriver plantations followed the spirit, if not exactly the letter, of Lafon's master plan.

At first the area was much less densely settled than its contemporary, the Faubourg Marigny, and often individuals would buy entire blocks as their country estates. There were large, detached houses along Annunciation Street near the river, and some as far back as Carondelet and Baronne streets. The proximity to the growing business district meant that eventually these private blocks would be bought and subdivided into smaller lots, where middle-class homes and rows of houses would be built.

Lafon's ambitious, semi-urban faubourg was the prototype for development that took place further upriver in the Garden District and beyond. It set a pattern of commuting to the downtown work environment from semirural upriver neighborhoods amidst a more open landscape. It also set the stage for the diverse mix of antebellum and postbellum architectural styles and types used throughout the Anglo-American "uptown" area. Since much of this faubourg's growth took place during the decades preceding the Civil War, two-story, galleried Greek Revival and Italianate (bracketed) townhouses predominate, and styles sometimes are eclectically combined in one structure. Decorative iron fences enclose landscaped lots of varying sizes. In addition there are fine examples of Creole cottages, raised center-hall villas, and several varieties of shotgun houses.

During the twentieth century some areas became badly run down but many fine buildings and gardens remain. The name Lower Garden District was coined in 1962 by architect and architectural historian Samuel Wilson, Jr., to describe its location below the Garden District. In 1972 the neighborhood was listed on the National Register of Historic Places, and preservation efforts, especially through the Preservation Resource Center and Operation Comeback, have shown signs of success in this important early neighborhood.

TOP RIGHT: Blaffer-Coleman house, 1869, Lewis Hilger, architect. This Italianate style house in the Coliseum Square area was restored in 1978 by Mr. and Mrs. James J. Coleman.. [119.1] RIGHT: The Bertucci-Schmaltz Building, built in 1870 at 1500–04 Magazine Street, is the headquarters for Operation Comeback. [119.2]

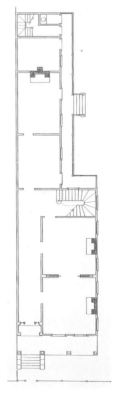

At left are the Gernon-Edwards-St. Martin house and the Fairchild Guest House on Prytania Street [119.3] and the floor plan for a typical two-story, galleried townhouse. [119.4] This plan is similar to the American townhouse, but it was usually built in suburban areas. Often made of wood and set back from the street behind a tree-shaded garden, they have two-story galleries in front and do not share party walls. Many had side-hall plans, but some of the larger houses had central halls. A favorite design-type utilized a combination of Greek Revival and Italianate details. Typically a box-like parapet above the cornice had a paneled design element, usually arched, but sometimes rectangular, and particularly popular in New Orleans.

GERNON-EDWARDS-ST. MARTIN HOUSE

1860; restored 1978, Monroe Labouisse, architect
Prytania Street, Lower Garden District

Front elevation.

OF ALL THE NEIGHBORHOODS AND HISTORIC DISTRICTS in New Orleans, none is more "classic" in one respect than the area now known as the Lower Garden District. Barthélémy Lafon's ambitious plan for subdividing the area immediately upriver from the Faubourg St. Mary was one of the first and most direct manifestations of the Greek Revival in New Orleans. Although many of its important features were never realized, the basic structure of the design and many of the classical street names have survived.

Prytania, one of the principal east-west streets in the plan, was originally named Rue de Prytanée, which referred to a prytaneum, or public building in ancient Greece. On Prytania Street between Terpsichore and Melpomene, Paul St. Martin III has restored a classic house type from this part of town and

Side hall entrance looking toward Prytania Street.

Gernon-Edwards-St. Martin House

A corner of the parlor/sitting room. Mary Ferry Bigelow was St. Martin's interior decorator.

made it one of the models for the renovation and restoration of his neighborhood. He and his architect, the late Monroe Labouisse, removed a concrete-block storefront that had unfortunately enclosed the lower segment of the side-hall double-galleried house. The style is transitional, part Greek Revival and part Italianate, a hybrid typical of New Orleans taste in the late-antebellum period.

The house was built by Michael Gernon about 1860 and purchased by William Edwards in 1866. A century later it was a run-down apartment house in a neighborhood that had become a tattered remnant of Barthélémy Lafon's Neoclassical vision. So desperate was the condition of the district, the Friends of the Cabildo selected it as the subject of the first volume of the *New Orleans Architecture* series, calling it "one of the

city's most threatened areas . . . in an extremely tenuous position . . . [requiring] immediate attention. . . ." The publication of that book coincided with the organization of the Coliseum Square Association in 1971, drawing attention to the area and galvanizing the residents' needs into preservation action. The district was soon included on the National Register and was one of the first in New Orleans to gain favorable tax status. By 1978 encouraging progress had been made, and young Paul St. Martin joined the fray, rescuing the dreary dwelling on Prytania and restoring its dignity and charm. St. Martin and his neighbors accepted a formidable challenge and continue to pursue the ambition of Lafon's plan for a distinctive, civilized, and convenient neighborhood near the heart of the New Orleans business district.

Double parlor, with rear area used as a dining room. St. Martin added a pair of French doors as access to the back ell of the house from this room. The fine original plasterwork is one of the reasons he chose this house to restore as his home.

The Toby-Westfeldt house is probably the oldest house extant in the Garden District. Originally owned by Thomas Toby, this raised cottage is now owned by Thomas D. Westfeldt. [124.1]

ABOVE: This 1857 house is the home of novelist Anne Rice and her husband, poet Stan Rice; it was the setting for The Witching Hour. *[124.2] BELOW: The Buckner house, on Jackson at Coliseum, as photographed c. 1858, one year after its completion. [124.3]*

Garden District

> *These mansions stand in the center of large grounds and rise, garlanded with roses, out of the midst of swelling masses of shining green foliage and many-colored blossoms. No houses could well be in better harmony with their surroundings, or more pleasing to the eye.*
> Mark Twain, *Life on the Mississippi,* 1883

The "Garden District" was a general phrase which originally referred to all of the fine, wooded, upriver residential area, including that now designated the Lower Garden District. The area specifically designated the Garden District today encompasses about eighty blocks and was part of the Livaudais Plantation, which was subdivided in the mid-1820s and incorporated in 1833 as part of the City of Lafayette. The term Garden District was in use by the middle of the century, about the time the area was annexed as the Fourth District of New Orleans, and was confirmed in the 1863 song, the "Garden District Waltz," dedicated to the "Ladies of the Fourth District."

The Garden District was Anglo-American with Creole influences; the Vieux Carré was French and Spanish Creole with American influences. Originally, of course, the Vieux Carré was strictly urban, downtown, the core of the city, whereas the Garden District was a suburb, uptown, from which many influential citizens commuted to their work at Canal Street and the Faubourg St. Mary.

Commuting and the growth of Lafayette and the new faubourgs above it was advanced in 1835, when the New Orleans and Carrollton Railroad began service on a line in the "neutral ground" along St. Charles Avenue (then Nayades Street), the main thoroughfare from Canal Street to the upriver resort village of Carrollton. (The entire path of the streetcar line was added to the National Register of Historic Places in 1973, officially recognizing its status as a signature element of New Orleans style, and several blocks of St. Charles Avenue as it passes through the Garden and Uptown districts were set aside as a locally designated historic district.)

By 1850, two years before it was annexed, Lafayette had a population of about 35,000 residents, most of whom lived in the working-class area between Magazine Street and the river, part of the neighborhood called the Irish Channel. North of Magazine Street was the upscale Garden District, known from the beginning for its architecture, landscaping, gardens, and other refinements.

In true American style, houses in the Garden District were set back from the street, at the center of shaded and bedded grounds surrounded by hedges, walls, and fences. The sites were rarely over an acre, but a notable exception was the James Robb house (c. 1857), now demolished, which dominated its entire three-and-one-half-acre city block and once served as Newcomb College. The streets were planted with shade trees, and in some ways it was like an Eastern Seaboard garden suburb or a New England village, with qualities characteristic of a subtropical climate.

The early houses showed an inclination towards frontal symmetry combined with an insistent verticality and were influenced by pervasive Creole conventions: front and side galleries, balconies, and ornamental cast iron for rails and fences; high-ceilinged double parlors with opulent large-scale plasterwork, wide floor-to-ceiling windows, French doors, and louvered blinds; and L-shaped formats with rear courtyards served by galleried dependencies similar to those found in the Vieux Carré. Anglo-American brick and wood were often used, as well as Creole stucco.

The concentration of antebellum architecture here, long counted among the attractions of the city, includes large, climate-sensitive, raised cottages and villas; double-galleried mansions with classical orders; rows of shotgun houses; a few Creole cottages; and a diversity of styles—especially Greek Revival (c. 1830–c. 1850) and Italianate (c. 1850–c. 1880), which were sometimes picturesquely combined in one structure. The works of a number of major architects are well represented. Among these are Henry Howard (1818–1884), James Gallier, Jr. (1827–1868), and the Frerets, William (1833–1911) and James (1838–1897), who lived in the district.

By the time the city of Lafayette was annexed by New Orleans in 1852, the Garden District was already a premier place to live, a distinction it has never lost as large-scale nineteenth-century homes have continuously been adapted for the twentieth century.

Lafayette Cemetery Number 1, established in 1833, is located in the Garden District. Well maintained, it has good examples of the above-ground burial architecture characteristic of flood-prone New Orleans. These are similar in design to the Creole tombs in the city, but the names on the tombs are predominately Anglo-American. This fusion, both in life and death, of Creole and American, Vieux Carré and uptown ways, is the classic style of this fascinating city as we have come to know it. Many tastes and temperaments have blended to form the individuality that New Orleans possesses, a true American *E Pluribus Unum* (one out of many). The Garden District, like the Vieux Carré, is a National Historic Landmark, and is also on the National Register of Historic Places (1971).

The James Robb house was built in 1857 on Washington Avenue and was the largest private house in New Orleans. Designed by James Gallier, Jr., it was later modified to house Newcomb College. The building was demolished in 1954. [125.1]

ABOVE: This raised cottage was built in 1874 by New Orleans writer George Washington Cable. The house is now owned by Mr. and Mrs. Charles S. Reily. Illustration by James Blanchard. [125.2] BELOW: Trinity Episcopal Church on Jackson Avenue, 1852–53, George Purves, builder-architect. The façade was rebuilt during the 1890s. Illustration by James Blanchard. [125.3]

PAYNE-FENNER-FORSYTH-STRACHAN HOUSE
1849–50
First Street, Garden District

MR. AND MRS. FRANK STRACHAN are only the second family line to own this house since Jacob U. Payne, a cotton merchant, built it. The second owner was Payne's son-in-law, Judge Charles E. Fenner. The William Bradish Forsyths purchased the house from the Fenner family and restored it; the Forsyths' daughter is Mrs. Strachan. The house is a Garden District landmark for numerous reasons, not the least of which is visual—its proud classical double gallery rising above the leafy green square it graciously commands. Its architectural beauty, however, is more easily discerned than its primary historical significance, which revolves around the Paynes' and Fenners' friendship with Jefferson Davis, president of the Confederacy, and his family. The Davises visited the Paynes often from Beauvoir on the Mississippi Gulf

Coast, and Varina (Winnie) Davis made her debut in this house and attended numerous Mardi Gras balls from here. On December 6, 1889, Jefferson Davis died in a corner bedchamber. (A large granite memorial commemorating Davis's death here was erected by the Ladies' Confederate Memorial Association in 1930.)

This house was included in Richard Pratt's popular *Treasury of Early American Homes*, with about a dozen other well-known New Orleans houses. Pratt wrote: "Ionic below and Corinthian above, the columns of this double gallery create an architectural effect familiar in the neighborhood, while indoors the woodwork and furnishings are notable, even for New Orleans." Little has changed since Pratt placed the house in that perspective more than forty years ago; if anything, time may have

OPPOSITE: Front elevation. This is one of the earliest Garden District houses with the classic elements of the neighborhood in place: a dignified, double-gallery colonnade facing the street and rising above grounds that constitute an enclosed formal garden.
ABOVE: Side elevation with formal rose garden. The double gallery places Ionic columns beneath Temple of the Winds Corinthian columns. The cast-iron capitals are marked New York, 1848. An ironwork-decorated side porch graces the stucco body of the brick mansion. Together these elements form a distinctive New Orleans architectural pattern.

added to its beauty. In 1949, the year Pratt's book was published, the architectural firm of Koch & Wilson renovated the rear wing; the firm also did work here in 1952, 1959, and lastly in 1960, when the garden pavilion (tea house) was added and the garden redesigned by the late

Umberto Innocenti, landscape architect.

Some accounts of the house say that Jacob Payne designed it himself. No record exists of either architect or builder, but a number of very competent builder-architects worked in the Garden District before and after the

Payne-Fenner-Forsyth-Strachan House

Civil War. Payne may very well have had one of them do it for him, as he closely oversaw construction progress.

Throughout the Garden District, there is a great unity of style and format in which discrete individual variations and improvisations were made—that is why it is an aesthetically harmonious neighborhood, with a characteristic and distinct sense of place. Indeed, the district is a National Historic Landmark because of the cumulative aesthetic quality and stylistic integrity represented by houses and gardens such as this.

TOP: Living room. The plan is a conventional four rooms over four, with a wide central hall on each floor. ABOVE: First floor bedchamber. This is the room in which Confederate President Jefferson Davis died December 6, 1889, while convalescing with the Fenners. RIGHT: From the dining room, looking into the parlor. Richard Pratt wrote in 1949: "The woodwork and furnishings are notable, even for New Orleans." This is no less true more than a generation later.

Payne-Fenner-Forsyth-Strachan House

GILMOUR-PARKER-EWIN-CHRISTOVICH HOUSE
1853, Isaac Thayer, architect and builder
Prytania Street, Garden District

IN THE DECADE BEFORE THE CIVIL WAR, London-born cotton broker Thomas C. Gilmour built this Italianate villa in the heart of the most elegant residential suburb in New Orleans, the American development that soon became known as the Garden District. Set back on a spacious lawn behind a decorative cast-iron fence and surrounded by flower beds, the house and its large corner lot epitomize the refined character of the neighborhood's nineteenth-century heyday.

The convenience of the New Orleans and Carrollton Railroad, which was built in 1835 on nearby St. Charles Avenue, inspired prosperous commuters like Gilmour to purchase country plots of a quarter of a square or more. The new suburbanites built dwellings of all sizes from mansions to cottages, but almost all were designed in the most fashionable style, and their spacious properties were

landscaped with exotic and native ornamental plantings.

The original Gilmour house, designed by Isaac Thayer, had a simple, six-room, three-over-three plan with a service ell, but in the late 1890s it was transformed with a flourish of up-to-date Eastlake additions and modifications by Mrs. John Parker, mother of John Milliken Parker, governor of Louisiana from 1920 to 1924. Nearly a century later, in 1985, when Mr. and Mrs. William K. Christovich purchased the house, they retained the city's most noted restoration architect, Samuel Wilson, Jr., to renovate the interior and exterior with consideration for the original form and style, its architectural evolution, and the modern needs and tastes of the new owners.

The stair hall had been changed in the 1898 renovations when the original stairs were removed, and a rear hall was added with an Eastlake staircase. Wilson re-

moved the later stairs and replicated the curved mahogany of the original 1850s style in the back hall. This left free space in the front hall for four closet areas, which he used for adding modern amenities. Wilson also conceived an elegant screen of columns to define the separate space of the rear hall and to indicate the era of Thayer's design.

Mary Louise Christovich, editor and one of the authors of the seven-volume *New Orleans Architecture* series, has been guided in furnishing the interiors by the 1866 Gilmour estate inventory.

Opposite: Entrance and side elevations. Italianate was the style of choice in the mid-nineteenth-century Garden District. A cast-iron veranda and balcony grace the asymmetrical form, which has evolved in three significant stages since the original 1853 design. Above: Sitting room. The interior decoration was influenced by extensive research in domestic inventories of the period, including that of the Gilmour estate. Left: Rear staircase from the entrance hall. The style of the original stair was reproduced in the 1986 renovations by Samuel Wilson, Jr.

Gilmour-Parker-Ewin-Christovich House

RODENBERG-GUNDLACH HOUSE

1853–54; addition in 1860s
Philip Street, Garden District

THE DEVELOPING AREA UPRIVER from the American Sector was a busy place in the decade before the Civil War. New Orleans commerce was still expanding, and houses for its growing class of prosperous entrepreneurs were being built right and left in the newly subdivided faubourgs; it was definitely not one of those places caricatured as a "sleepy time down South." After the wartime economic doldrums, the economy of the port regained some of its former health, and building activity resumed; new houses were built and additions were made to existing structures. Not all of the money for this activity was made in cotton or sugar. John H. Rodenberg, who dealt in grains down on New Levee Street, bought this corner property in 1852, the year the City of Lafayette became the Fourth District of New Orleans. Then it was a garden suburb, soon to be known by its descriptive sobriquet, the Garden District; today it is an urban neighborhood, a historic district, and still a busy place, full of life, and one of the most beautiful residential landscapes in America.

Rodenberg built a house characteristic of the district, a New Orleans townhouse type with a London plan of an interior side hallway, and outside, a formal double gallery with Greek Revival Corinthian columns above and Doric columns, classically correct in their simplicity, below. In the 1860s a two-story wing with two semi-octagonal bays was added, opening up the plan for more spacious possibilities inside; and outside it featured the opulence of Italianate ironwork and the more complicated surfaces preferred by post-Civil War taste.

An advertisement when Rodenberg sold the property in 1867 described it as "first class," much as it might be described today: "A beautiful brick residence in the Fourth District with handsomely improved garden, corner of Philip and Chestnut Streets." The description continued: "This dwelling is a splendidly built two-story attic brick, modern in all its finish and subdivisions, having on the front and side, verandas, built retired from the street. . . attached is a handsome garden, having a large variety of choice plants and vigorous shade trees. . . . This property is surrounded by first class improvements, neighborhood among the best in the Garden District, and the property unsurpassed for comfort, beauty, and durability."

Plus ça change, plus c'est la même chose (the more things change, the more they remain the same). The old French saying certainly applies to this American neighborhood and to this house, of which Sam Wilson, Jr., the city's leading architectural historian, wrote in 1954, a century after its construction: "The Borah house (it was then the residence of Judge and Mrs. Wayne G. Borah) is typical of the fine residences of the Garden District erected in the 1850s." Mrs. Borah is the daughter of Mr. and Mrs. David W. Pipes, who owned the house for more than fifty years. Mr. and Mrs. Harry Merritt Lane, Jr., acquired it in 1969 and made renovations to the house and garden. Susan Gundlach (formerly Mrs. Lane) and her husband James O. Gundlach currently occupy the house. They enlarged and updated the kitchen to accommodate the needs of their modern, active family, but made no changes to the exterior.

OPPOSITE: Front elevation. A classic Garden District house from the mid-nineteenth century, from entrance gate to side garden, beautifully preserved and restored. ABOVE: Entrance and garden detail. This is an old garden freshly landscaped, which continues the tradition of the place as described in 1867: A "handsome garden, having a large variety of choice plants and vigorous shade trees."

Rodenberg-Gundlach House

LEFT: Double parlors. The interiors were decorated by Sybil Favrot and Carolyn Howard to complement the opulent style of the interior architecture. TOP: Detail of parlor with superb plasterwork and glimpses of the garden through a bay window. ABOVE: Dining room. Ceilings are fourteen feet high.

ELKIN-HENDERSON-DERKS HOUSE

1859; renovated 1971, Douglas Freret, architect
Second Street, Garden District

JOAN CALDWELL has shown in her superb art history dissertation for Tulane University, "Italianate Domestic Architecture in New Orleans 1850–1880," that this picturesque style was the dominant fashion for houses in the city, especially in the Garden District, during a thirty-year era bracketing the Civil War. This romantic and luxurious style migrated to the city about 1850, only a few years after it was introduced in the eastern United States from England, but it remained a favorite here long after its popularity had waned elsewhere. The Gilmour-Christovich house on Prytania Street is an early New Orleans example.

The original builder of the Elkin-Henderson-Derks house is known to be Frederick K. Wing, a Philadelphia-born contractor, who constructed it for $12,000 in 1859 for Louis Elkin, the owner of a local carpet company. The identity of the architect is less certain. Henry Howard (1818–1884), who was born in Cork, Ireland, and came to Louisiana from New York City in 1837, became one of the outstanding architects in New Orleans and was linked through tradition with the design of this house. Howard practiced in the city from 1848 until his death in 1884, and his bold designs in the Italianate style and in handsomely detailed amalgamations of the Italianate and Greek Revival would certainly be compatible with the striking elevations of this house, which feature a projecting bay with arched windows, bold quoins, and almost baroque balconies overlooking the side garden.

Mr. and Mrs. Gerald Derks purchased the house in 1971 from the Hunt Hendersons, who had occupied it for sixty-four years. The Derkses totally renovated the entire house and the gardens, which contain many old plants and trees. The renovation architect was Douglas Freret. The landscape architect was Dorothy Hardie, and the interior decorator was Lucile Andrus.

Front elevation. The Italianate style transformed the Garden District during the period 1850–1880. This house has often been attributed to architect Henry Howard.

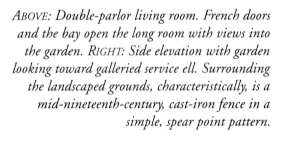

ABOVE: Double-parlor living room. French doors and the bay open the long room with views into the garden. RIGHT: Side elevation with garden looking toward galleried service ell. Surrounding the landscaped grounds, characteristically, is a mid-nineteenth-century, cast-iron fence in a simple, spear point pattern.

The dining room set for dinner. The Tudor Gothic style, linen-fold paneling was added in the early twentieth century, probably by the Hunt Hendersons, well-known art collectors who lived here from 1907 until the Gerald Derkses purchased the property in 19/1.

ROBINSON-JORDAN HOUSE
1862–66
Third Street, Garden District

THE PALATIAL SCALE of this luxurious Garden District mansion—the ceilings are sixteen feet high—reflects the grand aspiration of many mid-nineteenth-century Southerners for their region to rank among the great empires of the world. New Orleans, flush with the success of its port, had become the most cosmopolitan city in the South and the home of some of its most distinctive and ambitious architecture. In the Garden District, the most affluent of the suburbs, there are several palaces of that era, but the Robinson-Jordan house is an excellent representative, and the new wealth is expressed clearly and eloquently in its massive dimensions and elegant details. King Cotton politics and

ABOVE: Front elevation facing Third Street, behind a Neoclassical cast-iron fence. The sophisticated eclectic blend of Greek Revival and Italianate styles was popular in New Orleans for thirty years. OPPOSITE: Octagonal dining room (40' x 20') with ceiling frescoes by Dominique Canova and French wallpaper, "Scenic America," by Züber et Cie, Alsace, 1834, installed in 1940–41, during renovation.

Robinson-Jordan House

this domestic architecture, attributed to or at least influenced by James Gallier, Jr., (1827–1868) or Henry Howard (1818–1884), are sides of the same doubloon.

Antebellum New Orleans represents for many a quiet, static, Southern Camelot of a sort, when in fact, aside from its old Creole population, it was a "hot time" in a rapidly growing American town. Despite romantic notions conjured by the classical allusions of the architecture, the richness of materials, and sumptuous interior decorating, the Garden District today represents a more settled, established society than it did when it was a new suburb. Post-World War II prosperity and the passage of time make it seem more Old South now than ever it was before the Civil War. In *Southern Comfort* (1989) Frederick Starr described the frontier quality of the antebellum Garden District, where many of the original homes were built with fortunes assembled in the fragile boom and bust economy typical of most cities in that era. Some of the first residents were planters—"putting up a place in town"—but many more were merchants and few were native Southerners at all. Walter Grinnan Robinson was an exception. Robinson, born in Virginia, purchased the large building site at the corner of Third and Coliseum streets in 1857. This opulent house is a result of a fortune made in tobacco and banking.

Oddly, he began construction in 1862, during the Civil War, and completed it in 1866, an amazing accomplishment considering the privations most Southerners were suffering.

Double parlor-drawing room, to the left of the central hall, running the depth of the house, 27' x 42'. Ceiling frescoes are the originals, by Dominique Canova.

Robinson-Jordan House

Built of brick and plastered, the main body of the house faces the street, adorned with a classical double gallery with rounded ends. An L-shaped servants' wing with a carriage house, cast-iron balconies, and an octagonal bay extends from the rear, but was probably detached originally. The interiors are of a scale and architectural adornment practically unimaginable today. The original ceiling frescoes were by Dominique Canova.

Thomas Leslie Jordan, the pre-

sent owner, and his wife, Cornelia Ingersoll Jordan, purchased the property and restored the house in 1940–41. Their architect was Douglas V. Freret. The Jordans added the panoramic, hand-printed French wallpaper in the dining room (by Züber et Cie, Alsace, 1834) and furnished the house with antiques that are appropriate for the scale and architectural character of their Garden District mansion's mid-nineteenth century Italianate Neoclassicism.

Robinson-Jordan House

Garden District

MORRIS-ISRAEL-ARON HOUSE

c. 1868, Samuel Jamison, architect
First Street, Garden District

A PHOTOGRAPH OF THIS PICTURESQUE HOUSE is the title page illustration of *A Guide to New Orleans Architecture*, produced by the preservation-minded New Orleans Chapter of the American Institute of Architects. Its builder-architect, Samuel Jamison (1808–1880), is said to have lived here for a year before it was purchased by Joseph C. Morris. The house remained in the Morris family until 1921.

In 1967 Mr. and Mrs. Samuel Israel, Jr., restored the place entirely to its original beauty, removing interior and exterior alterations that had accumulated through the years. The Israels' architect was Edward B. Silverstein, the brother of Mrs. Israel (now Mrs. Aron). Some of the superb, lacy iron-work galleries produced locally by the Jacob Baumiller foundry had been enclosed. These now breathe free again as they mirror and embrace the green foliage of the neighborhood, harmonizing with the fine big trees and shrubs in the compound, which is enclosed by a cast-iron fence in a manner appropriate to this National Historic Landmark District.

The A.I.A. guide rightly recognized the significance of this Italianate villa, completed just after the Civil War as Garden District styles turned toward a rich but digni-

OPPOSITE: Front elevation. ABOVE: Garden elevation. French doors open onto a balcony and terrace. Garden District style combines elements in a uniquely New Orleans manner, part Creole and part Anglo-American.

fied romantic eclecticism. The *Daily Picayune* commented soon after it was completed: "The old-fashioned straight up and down box houses are, we are pleased to see, giving way to those more tasteful in design. . . . Among the most beautiful residences which have lately been erected in the Garden District is that of Mr. C. J. Morris, corner First and Coliseum. It is a two-story and attic brick stucco house . . . with octagonal wings, constructed with such regard to the unities that the eye is charmed at once. . . . The house was designed by Samuel Jamison, who has no superior as an architect in the South."

The architectural superiority of this house extends beyond the hand-carved front door into the privacy of the sumptuous interior. Inside are original features such as restored wall murals and a dining room ceiling canvas, rediscovered in the restoration, originally painted by an immigrant artist, Theobold Dreis. Other restored original aspects are intricate plasterwork, mantels, gold-leaf mirrors and curtain cornices, doors, hardware, and woodwork. This is a romantic Garden District house and garden *par excellence*—a rich symphony of New Orleans Italianate architecture and mid-nineteenth-century taste, beautifully replayed in our own day.

Opposite: Dining room. The original ceiling canvas, which had been painted in place by Theobold Dreis when the house was new, was rediscovered a century later in 1967 when the Israels restored the house. Above: Double parlors with original cornices, plasterwork, and mantels with petticoat mirrors.

Morris-Israel-Aron House

SORIA-FERRIER-MCCALL HOUSE
1875, Frederick Wing, architect
Prytania Street, Garden District

ON ITS PATH THROUGH THE GARDEN DISTRICT, Prytania Street is lined with trees, the black pickets of cast-iron fences, and the white columns of galleried houses. Typical of the colonnaded house-types that face the street is the Soria-Ferrier-McCall house, which shares the frontage of an entire block with only one other house. Early records indicate the two lots were purchased in 1845 by Winnifred Hubbard, a free woman of color also known as Winnie Undan. She had erected buildings on both lots before her death in 1862.

This lot was purchased from Hubbard heirs for $7,500 in 1868 by Cohen M. Soria, president of the Standard Guano Company and Standard Cotton Seed Oil Company. The older buildings on the lot were apparently demolished, and in 1875 architect Frederick Wing constructed this two-story, frame, Italianate house for the Sorias. It would remain in the family for 116 years. Wing also built a two-story frame carriage house on the rear of the property. In 1896 Cohen Soria's son, William, purchased the old raised villa next door, so for a brief time the two lots were owned once again by a single family.

The Italianate house was inherited by Mrs. Mae Soria Ferrier, daughter of William Soria, and was occupied by the Ferrier family for sixty-eight years. In 1969 Mae Ferrier's nephew, George Ferrier McCall inherited it, and it was occupied by his daughter and son-in-law, Mr. and Mrs. Philip E. Morehead. With the recent sale to Dr. and Mrs. Terry Creel, the property passed out of the family line for the first time since its construction.

The possession of a house by one family for so many years is rare, even in New Orleans. It is a tribute to the almost timeless nature of the Garden District, where the house stands in the shade of tall oak trees, a paragon of American suburban taste.

OPPOSITE: Entrance elevation on Prytania, set back from the ban-quette, behind a cast-iron fence. ABOVE: Dining room. A re-strained style, accented with family heirlooms, characterizes the interiors. BELOW: Screened side porch, a Southern outdoor living room, overlooking the carriage house and garden.

WILSON HOUSE AND KOCH & WILSON OFFICE

House, 1891; renovated in 1957–58, Samuel Wilson, architect; office adapted in 1973
Washington Avenue and Jackson Avenue at Magazine Street, Garden District

MAGAZINE is a lively, historic, and colorful commercial street of uptown New Orleans. *(Magasin* is French for warehouse or shop, a place to acquire provisions.) Since the nineteenth century its corridor has been a shopping district—there are dozens of antique shops; art galleries; interior decorating businesses; furniture, book, and grocery stores; and restaurants. As the traditional seam between the Garden District and the Irish Channel, Magazine Street also ties the Central Business District and Canal Street downtown to the Garden and Uptown districts.

On Washington Avenue just off of Magazine, near the edge of the Garden District and six blocks from his office, resides the embodiment and muse of classic New Orleans. Here is the home of Samuel Wilson, Jr., architect, scholar, author, teacher,

ABOVE: Wilson home. Side entrance façade. TOP: Living room, with dining room seen though pocket doors. The portrait in the living room is of the Rev. Benjamin Latrobe, ancestor of Mrs. Wilson. Over the dining room fireplace is a 1973 portrait of Samuel Wilson, Jr., by A. Ozols.

and citizen. From these two places have emanated the heartfelt and scholarly nurturing of the historic architectural soul of the city.

It seems entirely appropriate that Sam Wilson was married to the late Ellen Elizabeth "Betty" Latrobe, great-great-granddaughter of a genius of the early American architectural and engineering profession, Benjamin Henry Boneval Latrobe (1764–1820). They were married in Baltimore in 1951, the same year that Wilson published Latrobe's journals, *Impressions Respecting New Orleans.*

Sam Wilson's passion for architecture extended far beyond the normal limits of an occupation, and if anyone could be said to be the father of historic preservation in New Orleans, it is he, a native son, born here in the Carrollton District in 1911. (The "grandfather," then, would be

Richard Koch [1889–1971], Wilson's mentor and, in 1955, his partner in Koch & Wilson.) When Wilson received his degree in architecture from Tulane in 1931, "There just wasn't such a thing as historic preservation," he has recalled. After Wilson and Koch worked together in the 1930s for the Historic American Buildings Survey (HABS), however, they practically invented it as a local concept. Wilson's scholarly and intuitive opinions on historic preservation have since been held in high esteem. In 1950 he was the founding president of the Louisiana Landmarks Society, a pioneering preservation organization. Among his many publications is the introductory text for the *The Lower Garden District* (1971), volume one of *New Orleans Architecture.* Senior member of the firm of Koch & Wilson and a Fellow of the

ABOVE: The office of Koch & Wilson, Architects. TOP: Library. Over the mantel is an original copy of the superb Tanesse map of New Orleans (1817), one of a myriad of historical reference sources maintained at Koch & Wilson, which continues the architectural practice established as Armstrong & Koch in 1916.

American Institute of Architects, Wilson has served as architect on numerous restorations and renovations and has designed many new buildings.

He and Mrs. Wilson moved into their home in 1958, after he renovated the century-old gingerbread house (1891) to suit their needs. Its trimmed-up Shingle-Style lines—Victorian essence, only a suggestion of fuss—bespeak an understated and refined imagination. It represents a restrained yet comprehensive taste. His office, which he adapted for his firm in 1973 after Richard Koch's death, is only six blocks down Magazine Street at the downtown edge of the Garden District. The firm's name, Koch & Wilson, lives on, the past informing the present—as one would anticipate from Sam Wilson, Jr., scholarly gentleman, professional architect.

CATLEDGE HOUSE
1970; Myrlin McCullar, architect
Prytania Street, Garden District

MR. AND MRS. TURNER CATLEDGE built this house in 1970 in the heart of the Garden District across from Louis McGehee School. Their architect was the late Myrlin McCullar, whose own house is diagonally across Prytania at the corner of First Street. The site was available in this established district, in the garden of an earlier house razed during the 1960s.

Turner Catledge was originally from Philadelphia, Mississippi. He served as editor of the *New York Times* in the 1950s and 1960s, and retired to New Orleans with Mrs. Catledge in 1969, building this house with the approximate floor plan of their Manhattan apartment. Their interior decorator in New York and New

Orleans was Lucile Andrus. Together, Andrus and McCullar were able to accommodate the Catledges' furnishings and effect a smooth transition from the quintessential urban experience to the relative calm of Prytania Street.

The formal entrance façade of weathered stucco rises above a walled courtyard entered through piers and an iron gate. It seems comfortable on Prytania without exactly replicating historic Garden District architecture, and as a relatively new house in the context of a nationally known historic district, its restrained Regency style, with French doors opening into courtyard and side gardens, strikes just the right note of classic New Orleans.

OPPOSITE: *Front elevation. Architect McCullar interpreted the European background of New Orleans architecture with this courtyard entrance.* ABOVE: *Living room, overlooking the rear courtyard garden.* LEFT: *Entrance stair hall. Interior decorator Lucile Andrus worked with client and architect to decorate the Catledges' New Orleans home in the spirit of their New York apartment.*

Catledge House

Howard-McAshan House

1932–33, Richard Koch, architect, Koch & Armstrong
St. Charles Avenue, St. Charles Avenue District

RICHARD KOCH WAS BORN IN NEW ORLEANS in 1889 and was graduated in architecture from Tulane University in 1910. He went on to study at the École des Beaux-Arts in Paris from 1911 to 1912 and then began an apprenticeship with Aymar Embury II in New York City, later working with John Russell Pope. Koch returned to New Orleans in 1916 and joined with Charles Armstrong to form Armstrong & Koch, a partnership which continued until 1935, during which time he designed this house on St. Charles Avenue.

Preservation and historical survey projects in the 1920s and 1930s helped Koch appreciate American regional architecture; he was the restoration architect for the famous Louisiana antebellum homes, Shadows-on-the-Teche in New Iberia, in 1922, and Oak Alley Plantation

near Vacherie, in 1926. During the Depression he supervised the Historic American Buildings Survey projects in Louisiana, measuring and photographing with great zeal.

Out of these experiences, he began to synthesize regional domestic architecture for his own designs. From French, Spanish, and English Colonial, and Creole and other vernacular idioms, Koch evolved a personal, creative, and romantic, yet academic eclecticism to solve design problems for his own day. (In 1947, for the Simon & Schuster book, *Your Solar House*, Koch provided a conservatively modern design, which he described in this way: "The principles which are basic in what today is known as solar housing are not new to the South; the development of the idea in Louisiana is the history of the early architecture of the state, a style borrowed largely

from the West Indies.") Restoration, adaptive reuse, and new work sometimes practically merged in one building in his beautiful and innovative work.

For Mrs. Harry Turner Howard, whose husband made a fortune administering a state-chartered lottery company, Richard Koch synthesized American Georgian, French Colonial, and Creole domestic architecture into a large house set behind a high brick wall. Allison and Kenneth McAshan, the present owners, are noted arts patrons and collectors who value the privacy of the large lot and the style that Koch undoubtedly derived in part from the rear elevation of Shadows-on-the-Teche, a vernacular melding of American and French colonial influences. The McAshans appreciate Richard Koch's work of architectural art and preserve the spirit of the place in form and detail.

Howard-McAshan House

LEFT: *Dining room with view into stair hall.* ABOVE: *Stair hall.*

Howard-McAshan House

Magazine Street at Second, 1947. Except for the streetcar tracks, which have been removed, this street scene today would show little change over the last half-century, reflecting the architectural stability of this Irish Channel neighborhood. [160.1]

ABOVE and BELOW The Bogart-Filson cottage was built by Isaac Bogart in 1849–50, with George Purves as architect. It is currently owned by Ronald C. Filson, former dean of the Tulane University Architecture School. [160.2 and 160.3]

Irish Channel District

Traditionally in uptown New Orleans, working-class neighborhoods developed near and parallel to the commercial and industrial riverfront. Away from the river this pattern graduates to middle-class areas near Magazine Street, followed by more affluent neighborhoods toward St. Charles Avenue. Beyond St. Charles the tendency reverses, as poorer neighborhoods were built on less desirable, lower elevation property.

The working-class mirror of the Garden District is the Irish Channel District, which historically began with a largely Irish immigrant community near the warehouses in Faubourg St. Mary, and grew upriver between Magazine Street and the docks. The Irish Channel has long been a proud, working-class neighborhood. Its primary growth came during the mid-nineteenth century and is reflected by many simple—but not unornamented—houses, including rows of identical single and double shotgun and camelback (a second story added at the rear) shotgun cottages with small front yards and larger rear gardens with service areas. This 104-block district also contains churches, schools, commercial buildings (especially along Magazine Street), and warehouses. The area is rich in late-nineteenth-century architecture. Greek Revival, Italianate, and various Victorian styles predominate.

To this day the Irish Channel District has the scale, the texture, and atmosphere of a late-nineteenth-century neighborhood, with modest but comfortable houses set in tidy yards, behind decorative fences and trimmed hedges. Historically, the Irish Channel was the birthplace of many jazz musicians of German, French, Irish, and Italian descent. All members of the Original Dixieland Jazz Band, the first jazz band to make a phonograph record and the first to go to Europe, were from this district. As an Architectural District of the National Register of Historic Places (1976), the Irish Channel District boundaries are: Tchoupitoulas Street, Jackson Avenue, Delachaise Street, and Magazine Street.

Revitalization, community spirit, and a "neighborhood watch" are lead by a neighborhood improvement association. Clay Square, which dates from the 1830s when it was named in honor of U.S. Senator Henry Clay of Kentucky, has been completely renovated by the Parks and Parkways Commission. Operation Comeback, as in the adjacent Lower Garden District, is offering low-interest financing to encourage new residents to the Channel to buy and renovate houses in this conveniently located district of homeowners.

An early surviving landmark of the area now known as the Irish Channel District is the Grigson-Gerhard-Sanders-Didier house. (See following pages.) Its front and rear columned galleries and spacious grounds remind one of the days when there were plantations on this fertile land at the Mississippi levee.

GRIGSON-GERHARD-SANDERS-DIDIER HOUSE

1835
Seventh Street, Irish Channel District

THIS ANTIQUE TWO-STORY FRAME HOUSE—with its graceful, fanlighted late-Federal style doorway, West Indian roof line with two delicate dormers, and galleries with simple boxed columns front and rear—actually predates the surrounding neighborhood that qualified this area as a historic district. (Most of the buildings in the Irish Channel District were constructed between 1850 and 1900.) It is a local landmark in its own right, standing on a large, level plot near the Mississippi levee—as it has since right after the subdivision of the Jacques Livaudais plantation. It is near the one-block-long Livaudais Street in that part of the city of Lafayette where the Livaudais plantation house (demolished 1863) had stood between Washington Avenue and Sixth Street.

Stylistically the house is more reminiscent of coastal Carolina or the Feliciana parishes than a small New Orleans plantation, but in Carolina the second-story door

North elevation. Built soon after the area became the Faubourg Livaudais, this house predates most development in the Irish Channel.

would not be French and the gallery would be called a *piazza*. The charming, though incongruous, house was built by Mary Ann Grigson in 1835, soon after she bought the land. Before the Civil War it became the property of the Gerhard family, which owned it until 1962. The architect Charles F. Sanders renovated it as his home in the late-1970s, recognizing the potential of its architectural integrity. Not only was the exterior relatively intact, but surviving inside were the original staircase,

beamed ceilings, mantelpieces, and paint colors (though hidden beneath many subsequent layers). The present owner, James D. Didier, a nationally known dealer and expert in nineteenth-century Americana, has furnished the house to complement the architecture and made further refinements in the restoration with the continued interest of Sanders and consultations with H. Parrott Bacot, an expert on early Louisiana cultural history. Didier maintains the perfect, rural garden setting Sanders began for the house, which in its modern context is near an industrial area.

When the Irish Channel neighborhood was listed on the National Register of Historic Places in 1976, this house stood in a large patch of weeds, forlorn and haunted-looking. Could anyone see the house today and doubt the beneficial progress of historic preservation and historic district designation? There are notable successes like this all over New Orleans, but, as with any good story, it is the cast of characters, the people like Chuck Sanders and Jim Didier who move into an old neighborhood, providing new leadership and energy, investing the sweat of their brows, that make it come to life. If Mary Ann Grigson is sometimes a ghost on her original old staircase, she should be a peaceful, happy spirit come home to rest (and make a joyful noise) in a familiar and well-loved place.

ABOVE: Living room. An expert collaborative restoration by an architect, an antique dealer, and a museum consultant that interprets the simple, late-Federal architecture. LEFT: Upstairs bedchamber. No ghost along the Mississippi from the photographs of Clarence John Laughlin could possibly be anything but an elegant apparition in such surroundings. Mosquito netting such as this protected sleeping citizens from the pesky and disease-carrying insects before window screens and air conditioning were invented.

Grigson-Gerhard-Sanders-Didier House

GAINES-THELIN COTTAGE

1850s; renovated 1971
Sixth Street, Irish Channel District

A BLOCK AWAY FROM MAGAZINE STREET toward the river is the Irish Channel home of Philip Panchaud de Bottens Thelin, who restored and renovated this cottage in 1971. Thelin, who came to the city as a banker, restored his first New Orleans house at 904 Louisiana Avenue. He bought this Sixth Street house as a restoration project and investment. It was a "hippy house," he says, but it still had many of its original features, including servants' quarters and a fig orchard in back. After he took early retirement from banking and went into real estate, he moved here.

Early residents of the City of Lafayette frequently purchased large corner lots in order to have space for outbuildings, vegetable and flower gardens, orchards, and even small pastures. Typical was the 1847 purchase by Charles Clark Gaines of five lots at the corner of Sixth and Live Oak (today, Constance) streets, in the heart of the subdivided village.

Gaines apparently built this center-hall cottage in the Greek Revival style with an overlay of Italianate bracketing in the early 1850s. It sits near the sidewalk with a

cast-iron picket fence separating the public and private spaces, protecting a quiet front garden that consists largely of clipped shrubs. Gaines was listed in the New Orleans City Directory as an "importer of foreign and domestic hardware," and it is possible he imported the unusually intricate, grapevine-patterned, cast-iron gallery railing. Although grapevine patterns were popular in mid-nineteenth-century New Orleans, this particular one seems to be unique in the city.

As Phil Thelin was restoring the interiors of the cottage, he found original stencilled and hand-painted wall surfaces in the dining room. Five years later he discovered the ceiling also had hand-painted designs. Today the walls and ceiling of the dining room appear in all their nineteenth-century glory. These touches complement the sophisticated European furnishings, which include a fine tapestry that is framed by the stencilling as though the two decorations were intended for each other.

Phil Thelin is justifiably proud of his distinctive Irish Channel home, which he rescued from dilapidation and carefully restored to its original dignity.

OPPOSITE: Front elevation. One of the Irish Channel's finest classical cottages. ABOVE: Dining room. Thelin restored this interior in the 1970s. He has decorated his cottage largely with inherited furnishings and art objects.

Gaines-Thelin Cottage

Evariste Blanc house, Bayou St. John, an early nineteenth-century Creole-French plantation house. [166.1]

Faubourg Tremé. A row of frame, double cottages once stood on the site of the Municipal Auditorium parking lot. The illustration was drawn in 1844 by Surgi. [166.2]

Villa Meilleur, 1440 Governor Nicholls Street, Tremé. c. 1828. This house is being restored as the center for the Tremé Historical Education Network. John C. Williams and Arthur Q. Davis, restoration architects [166.3].

Esplanade Ridge District

Esplanade Avenue, handsomely landscaped with sycamores and live oaks, was the fashionable avenue for antebellum Creole promenades—the *promenade publique*—and thus the French equivalent of St. Charles Avenue in the American Garden District. Connecting the French Quarter to City Park at Bayou St. John, Esplanade Avenue became the great nineteenth-century suburban boulevard of Creole New Orleans.

The first seven blocks of Esplanade Avenue are on land that was the eastern band of the City Commons that surrounded the eighteenth-century town. The name *Esplanade* came from the parade ground, or esplanade, at Fort St. Charles, at the river and one of the five forts positioned at the ramparts around the city. In 1810 surveyor Jacques Tanesse laid out the new avenue from the river to Rampart Street, parallel to Canal Street on the other side of the Quarter. By the next year houses were already being advertised for sale. In 1822 surveyor Joseph Pilie introduced a plan to extend the avenue all the way to Bayou St. John, but ten years passed before the city resolved to attempt it. In 1841 the avenue was open as far as the intersection with Bayou Road, and by 1850 it reached the bayou. The avenue took forty years to complete and cut across more than thirty small plantations from Rampart Street to Bayou St. John.

As the French Quarter became more crowded and declined in status, many prominent Creole families moved to Esplanade Avenue and built fine homes. Two-story, galleried, side-hall houses, not unlike those in the Lower Garden District, are a constant early type, dressed out in various styles and periods. As this was indeed a fashionable boulevard, there are few shotgun cottages, but all of the other characteristic New Orleans models are present, both Anglo-American and the local amalgamations. Adjacent historic Creole neighborhoods, including the faubourgs Marigny (a district in its own right), Tremé, New Marigny, St. John, and Pontchartrain, however, are filled with cottages and smaller-scaled dwellings. The avenue commences at the Greek Revival United States Branch Mint (1835), built near the river and a part of the Vieux Carré, and ends at the Beaux-Arts New Orleans Museum of Art (1911) at City Park. Along its length, practically an entire architectural history of Orleans Parish is concentrated. Almost any type, style, and period found elsewhere in the city, including late-eighteenth- and early nineteenth-century French Colonial plantation houses, such as the Pitot House (c. 1799) at Bayou St. John, can be seen here. There is an important cemetery at the northern end of the district,

St. Louis Cemetery Number 3, which displays the elaborate above-ground funerary art and architecture characteristic of the city.

The Esplanade Ridge District is one of the largest local historic districts in New Orleans, covering 250 blocks from the Vieux Carré to Bayou St. John, and includes the important Faubourg Tremé. Claude Tremé had sold a few lots from his plantation as early as 1798, and in 1810, as Esplanade Avenue was laid out on the eastern commons, the city bought Tremé's plantation, combined it with the northern commons, and subdivided it. This was the first faubourg subdivision undertaken by the city government. Lots sold rapidly and farms along Bayou Road farther north were soon being developed as well, expanding as far as North Claiborne Avenue by 1841, with a population primarily made up of French and Spanish Creoles and free people of color. Creole cottages from the 1830s to the 1850s, usually with double-dormer windows, are the most common house-types. One of the faubourg's most important landmarks is St. Augustine's Church (1841–42), designed by Jacques N. B. de Pouilly, and built on Governor Nicholls Street at St. Claude.

The National Register boundaries of the broad Esplanade Ridge District were established in 1980. The farther out in the district one goes, the larger the lots and the more Victorian in style the houses become. Except for U.S. 90 there are few modern intrusions, and of over four thousand buildings, only about three hundred are non-historic. The district has both a preservation and a civic association leading its renewal; this is urbane—rather than urban—renewal, in keeping with the Esplanade's Creole past.

ABOVE: Faubourg Tremé. St. Augustine's Church, on Governor Nicholls Street, between North Rampart and St. Claude streets; photograph c. 1885. [167.1] BELOW: This 1861 Italian villa near Esplanade Avenue was designed by James Gallier, Jr., and Richard Esterbrook for Florence A. Luling, a wealthy cotton merchant. The modern illustration is by James Blanchard. [167.2]

Bruneau-Bynum cottages. These three-bay shotgun cottages are typical of Faubourg Tremé. They were built by Joseph Bruneau about 1850 and restored in 1986 by Adolph F. Bynum, Jr., a dedicated preservationist. [167.3]

MAYOR JAMES PITOT HOUSE

c. 1799; restoration begun 1964, Koch & Wilson, restoration architects
1440 Moss Street, Esplanade Ridge District

Front elevation. The only French Colonial style plantation house on Bayou St. John that is open to the public. Restored by the Louisiana Landmarks Society as its headquarters, it is furnished and landscaped to represent the period of James Pitot's ownership, c. 1810–19.

THE BAYOU ST. JOHN NEIGHBORHOOD of the Esplanade Ridge Historic District has a number of outstanding late-eighteenth- and early-nineteenth-century architectural landmarks on Moss Street. In addition to the Pitot House Museum are: the Blanc-Erlanger house (the Sanctuary) at 924; the Spanish Custom House at 1300; and the Evariste Blanc house (Holy Rosary Rectory) at 1342.

The first French settlement in the New Orleans area was established here in 1708, ten years before La Nou-velle-Orléans was officially founded over on the Mississippi. The Bayou Road, an ancient portage along the ridge between Bayou St. John and the Mississippi River, formed the spine along which eighteenth-century plantations were located. Eventually, many of the large concessions between New Orleans and Lake Pontchartrain, granted by the Company of the Indies and the French and Spanish crowns, were subdivided into smaller *habitations* (plantations).

In 1799 Spaniard Don Bartholémé Bosque began

Salon or drawing room. French doors open onto the second floor gallery from a room finished in a New Orleans or Creole style of the early American republic. The box mantlepiece, of Louisiana cypress, is French Creole Federal in style, and similar to others found in the city c. 1800.

construction of this galleried, French colonial style plantation house, but sold it to Frenchman Joseph Reynes in 1800. It was completed by Vincent Rillieux's widow (Edgar Degas's great-grandmother), who bought it in 1805; her builder was Hilaire Boutté. In 1810 Mme. Rillieux sold it to James Pitot (1761–1831) who was the first elected mayor of the incorporated city of New Orleans after the Louisiana Purchase. Pitot's *habitation* was thirty acres, and he considered it a country house.

A series of families owned the place from 1819 until

it was purchased in 1904 by Mother Frances Cabrini (St. Frances Cabrini, the first American saint), whose Missionary Sisters of the Sacred Heart and Cabrini High School donated it to the Louisiana Landmarks Society in the early 1960s for removal and restoration nearby. In 1964 the Society moved the house from 1370 Moss Street to the present site (about 200 feet). Restoration has been an ongoing project over the years since, and in 1973 the house was opened to visitors for tours. The Pitot House Museum is now the headquarters of the society, a

Mayor James Pitot House

Ground floor dining room. The 1848 portrait by Adolph Rinck is an example of the French Academic School so popular in early Louisiana. A French door leads to the front parterre garden. The punkah (shoo-fly fan) over the dining table dates from c. 1790.

vanguard of historic preservation founded in the 1950s.

The architectural firm Koch & Wilson, particularly Samuel Wilson, Jr., was in charge of moving the house and restoring it. Guidance for the restoration was gleaned from the building itself, old sketches and descriptions, and the firm's knowledge of the architecture of the period. The house has been furnished with Louisiana and American decorative arts from the early 1800s when Mayor Pitot owned the property.

Pitot, a Frenchman originally from Normandy, arrived in New Orleans from Saint-Domingue (Santo Domingo) after the slave rebellion there. Except for details of the Federal style salon, which overlooks the bayou, Pitot House is similar in many ways to the elegantly functional raised houses he would have known in the West Indies.

The house is listed on the National Register of Historic Places and has been designated a landmark by both the Orleans Parish and New Orleans historical commissions. The Louisiana Landmarks Society has established a Pitot House Endowment Fund solely to insure its preservation.

Ground floor office off the front gallery. James Pitot was in the international import-export business and, in the Creole tradition, may have had an office at home. Bayou St. John then was an important part of the New Orleans port system.

Mayor James Pitot House

BLANC-LABATUT-PARKER-ERLANGER HOUSE
The "Sanctuary"
c. 1800
Moss Street, Esplanade Ridge District

THE SANCTUARY has been the home of Mr. and Mrs. Benjamin Erlanger since 1973–74 when they renovated it as their residence. Benjamin Erlanger commented: "We have sought to re-create the feeling of its early times without attempting a museum-type restoration. We have replaced concrete flooring at the ground level with old brick [and] resurrected old marble and old tiles beneath the concrete and reinstalled them as fireplace hearths. We installed central heating and air conditioning without sac-

rificing ceiling heights. We removed the existing kitchen in the house and converted the adjacent 1927 garage for the purpose, following the practice of bygone times of not having the kitchen in the main house."

The Erlangers have successfully re-created the spirit of "bygone times" along Bayou St. John in their sanctuary. But they are not the first to have appreciated the charm of the place as a home. From 1926 to 1950 the house belonged to Walter Parker, a leading figure in the

rehabilitation of Bayou St. John in the 1930s and 1940s. He and his wife made many additions to the property. Two new outbuildings were built, including the garage that is now the kitchen. In the main house, a handsome, mahogany interior spiral stair was crafted following the expert design of architect Moise Goldstein, in a style that accords well with the surrounding structure. (The original exterior stair in the rear gallery was removed.) Bath facilities were created on each floor, and the attic became a useful space for the first time.

The two-and-a-half-story plantation house, a galleried Creole type with Anglo-American influence (it has a center-hall floor plan and Federal style woodwork), was probably built by Louis Antoine Blanc (1758–1825) sometime after 1793, when he purchased the property extending from the bayou toward what is now Esplanade Avenue. Construc-

Opposite: Garden elevation. The grounds, enclosed by a cast-iron fence, have large oaks and palms, as well as a variety of fruit trees, including fig, banana, pomegranate, papaya, and persimmon. Top: View from the main house toward the garage addition, which is now the kitchen wing. Above: Stair hall. This staircase was built during the renovations of the 1920s and 1930s, replacing an exterior staircase in the rear gallery.

tion is on brick pyramid foundations. The first story is of plaster-covered brick; the second of brick-between-posts, covered with boards. The hipped roof has dormers and is topped by a widow's walk, and the two-story gallery is supported by Doric columns on the first floor and slender colonettes on the second. There are four rooms, unequal in size, off of a center hall, but the overall appearance is Creole.

From the 1830s until 1846 the Louis Blanc property was owned by the city of New Orleans, and the house served as a boys' orphanage from 1836 to 1840. In 1859 Felix Labatut, a merchant and outstanding citizen, purchased the house. Later Charles Louque, a distinguished attorney and Confederate veteran resided here. For generations it has been a safe sanctuary, indeed, even an orphanage, sheltering in its big, bold Creole-style simplicity, people who have called it home.

FLEITAS-CHAUFFE-REEVES HOUSE
c. 1802; upper floor moved in 1835
Bayou Road, Esplanade Ridge District

OPPOSITE: Entrance elevation. ABOVE: Sitting room.

IN HIS DELIGHTFUL BOOK *Frenchmen, Desire, Good Children, and Other Streets of New Orleans*, John Chase described Bayou Road: "This portage, this established and maintained way of intercommunication, this dean of all New Orleans streets [is] older than them all and older that the city itself." The road was probably first an animal path, then an Indian portage, then Le Chemin au Bayou St. Jean to the French, El Camino al Gran Bayou Llamado San Juan to the Spanish, and finally, and simply, Bayou Road. During the colonial period, *habitations* (plantations) fronted on Bayou Road from the ramparts of the city to the bayous.

In 1802 Domingo Fleitas acquired an *habitation* from Carlos Guadioli, who had received a Spanish grant for the land the previous year. Fleitas may have built the house at that time. When Esplanade Avenue was extended into this area in the mid-nineteenth century, it bisected numerous *habitations* that fronted on Bayou Road. The farm house of the widow Fleitas lay directly in the path of the extension. Archival records indicate the upper story of the house was moved to its present location in 1835 by Jean Manuel Fleitas, son of Domingo Fleitas. Originally the house had two stories, a wooden dwelling above a brick first floor, but when the top floor was removed it was set on low brick piers, and a kitchen wing was added to the rear. The interior was renovated at this time with Greek Revival woodwork. The steeply pitched hipped roof with dormers, the hall-less French colonial floor plan, the hardware, the shuttered French doors, and the front and rear galleries with colonettes are all characteristic of the colonial period.

In 1901 the house was purchased by Henry S. Chauffe, who enlarged it with a wing on one side and a bay on the rear. The Chauffe family occupied the place until 1977, when Cynthia Reeves bought it and restored the house to emphasize its Creole character. Today, well within the modern New Orleans city limits, the Fleitas-Chauffe-Reeves house evokes a quiet, colonial roadside charm.

Fleitas-Chauffe-Reeves House

CABIRAC-TREPAGNIER-VILLA COTTAGE

1893; exterior remodeled 1935
Moss Street, Esplanade Ridge District

ABOVE: Entrance elevation. The style of the Villa cottage is New Orleans eclectic, from the odd coexistence of plantation mansion and shotgun cottage features, to the wonderfully provocative interior decoration. The landscape architecture is by Robert Truxilto.
OPPOSITE: This table-sculpture is called Circus.

NESTLED BESIDE THE 1835 EVARISTE BLANC plantation house on Moss Street facing Bayou St. John, is the late-nineteenth-century shotgun cottage of Mario Villa. On a small lot subdivided from the old, bayou-front *habitation,* Barthélémy Cabirac built the original Italianate cottage. In 1935 Mr. and Mrs. Henry Trepagnier purchased the cottage and renovated it, perhaps to fit more compatibly with its neighbors and evoke the atmosphere of the plantation setting. They rebuilt the front gallery with Doric box columns and an ornate cast-iron railing, gabled the front of the old hipped roof, enlarged the interior space by enclosing the side and rear galleries, and re-

placed the wooden picket fence with antique cast iron.

In 1989 Villa, a Managua-born artist, bought the cottage and transformed the interiors with his creative furnishings. The youthful virtuoso, who studied at Tulane University in architecture and archaeology, was quoted in a 1988 *Southern Accents* article: "I wanted to be an architect-artist who designs art that is furniture." He established his gallery on Magazine Street in 1983, representing his own work and that of other artists, and in 1985 he produced his first Neoclassical-romantic furniture-sculpture, which is now internationally known and collected.

Cabirac-Trepagnier-Villa Cottage

LEFT: *Front and rear sitting rooms. The marble mantels, imported from France, were added by Mr. and Mrs. Charles René Therelle, owners of the cottage in the 1960s. The interior decoration is uniquely Mario Villa—a mixture of his own creations and acquired objects.* TOP: *Dining room. Each room in the Villa cottage is like a stage set.* ABOVE: *A corner of the cottage furnished with numerous pieces of Villa's work, much of it welded steel.*

DUNBAR-BRADEN HOUSE

c. 1875
Esplanade Avenue, Esplanade Ridge Historic District

OPPOSITE: Front elevation. Except for a missing balustraded front porch, removed before the Bradens' renovation, the Second Empire style of this distinctive house helps preserve the flavor of nineteenth-century Esplanade Avenue. ABOVE: Den, with glimpse of the impressive original staircase and other opulent features of the spacious entrance hall.

ESPLANADE AVENUE, the great nineteenth-century suburban boulevard of Creole New Orleans, became the French equivalent of St. Charles Avenue in American New Orleans above Canal Street. By 1850 the avenue had been completed from the Vieux Carré to Bayou St. John, and prominent Creole families were building fashionable homes along its tree-shaded way. Eventually, Esplanade Avenue became a veritable showcase for distinctive, as well as locally traditional, architectural styles and types.

Esplanade developed northward, over time, from the eighteenth-century French Quarter, so that farther out the avenue the architecture is increasingly Victorian in character. Neat landscaped lawns surrounded by iron picket fences predominate. The Dunbar-Braden house exemplifies the surviving spirit of the avenue. It was built in 1875 for George Washington Dunbar in the stylish mansard mode of Second Empire France. Originally, its nearly identical twin stood next door, occupied by Dunbar's son and his family. In 1879, after his father died, George Hacker Dunbar moved into this house, which his family occupied until 1925.

The present owners, Mr. and Mrs. Henry E. Braden IV, are active preservationists. Mrs. Braden is chairman of the Historic Districts Landmarks Commission and an interior decorator who emphasizes historical aspects of taste. The Bradens' home demonstrates her preservation and professional interests.

The raised cottage is found throughout mid-nineteenth-century New Orleans neighborhoods, especially in suburban areas where there were large lots, like the Garden District and farther uptown neighborhoods and along Esplanade Avenue. Raised on brick walls or high piers, these handsome frame houses usually had a wide veranda along the front, which sometimes wrapped around the sides. They were embellished with details from Greek Revival, Italianate, or combinations of the two styles. The Rice-Williams house on Camp Street (page 184) is an excellent example of the Anglo-American center-hall plan. [182.1 and 182.2]

ABOVE: The Bullitt-Neitzschman house, a Swiss chalet design, was built in 1868–69 on Carondelet Street. [182.3] BELOW: The colorful, eclectic, Willems house on Palmer Avenue is from the mid-1870s. [182.4]

Uptown District

This upriver district is composed of residential suburbs subdivided from the eighteenth- and nineteenth-century plantations and faubourgs that bordered on the Mississippi above Lafayette and extended toward the back-of-town swampy woods. By 1850 part of the area had been incorporated as Jefferson City, which was later absorbed into the Sixth Municipal District of New Orleans along with other faubourgs all the way to Carrollton. One of the largest districts on the National Register of Historic Places, containing about 750 blocks and over 10,700 structures, Uptown is roughly bounded by Louisiana Avenue, Tchoupitoulas by the levee, Lowerline Street at Carrollton, and Claiborne Avenue toward Lake Pontchartrain.

Uptown is a common reference for the areas above Canal Street, but it was never the name of a particular neighborhood. Since this historic district was made up of many neighborhoods, the general term "uptown" was used to describe it. Neighborhood associations within the district are often named for the early faubourgs, such as Bouligny, Rickerville, and Hurstville. The area around Tulane University, Newcomb College, and Loyola University is most often called the University Section.

The area above Lafayette remained mostly rural even after the incorporation of Jefferson City. Although maps from the era show sprawling faubourgs fanning toward the river, these were, for the most part, only lines on paper. When the district was annexed in 1870, it was still primarily a sparsely settled village with small Creole cottages and a number of larger homes. The New Orleans and Carrollton Railroad, which began running in 1835 along St. Charles Avenue, eventually provided impetus to suburban growth, but significant development did not begin in the upriver portions of the district until the late 1880s as large Victorian homes began to appear. At that time the area was generally considered a part of the Garden District. In 1886 the prominent architect Thomas Sully built his residence at 4010 St. Charles in the hybrid Victorian style, Queen Anne, that he used for a number of other houses in the area. By the 1890s the empty blocks between Jefferson Avenue and Audubon Park were rapidly filling, and at the turn of the century St. Charles Avenue near the park was the center of fashionable development. Building a few blocks north of St. Charles toward the lake was held back because of the low elevations, but by 1910 and into the 1920s the area was drained and filled and development was dramatic. Large, fine houses were built nearest St. Charles Avenue, while middle-income housing began to spread toward the dairy and truck farms on that side of town.

Every socioeconomic group is represented in the architecture of the Uptown District, but there is a large representation of upper-middle class and the even more affluent, who usually employed architects to design their houses. Audubon Place was one of the most exclusive neighborhoods. Established in the early 1890s, it has a seriously chic Beaux-Arts ambience. The oldest surviving structures in the Uptown District are near Louisiana Avenue and the river, but since development was scattered and took several generations to complete, a great variety of styles exist side by side, including: Creole, Greek Revival, Italianate, Queen Anne, Eastlake, California Bungalow, Gothic, Mission, Craftsman, Prairie, Art Nouveau, and Colonial and other revivals. Single and double shotgun cottages are numerous.

Lots in the Uptown District are usually of generous size and most houses have front yards. The twentieth-century suburban setting is confirmed by driveways for automobiles, garages, and some swimming pools. The streets are tree-shaded, the pace is relaxed, and touches of local taste in iron work, galleries, French doors, and rear courtyard gardens create an atmosphere that is unmistakably New Orleans.

Greenville Hall, on St. Charles Avenue, was built in 1882 and served as part of St. Mary's Dominican College. It now houses part of the Loyola University Law School. [183.1]

ABOVE: The entrance to Audubon Place in 1895, showing the landscaped median and glimpses of the first two houses in the exclusive development. [183.2] BELOW: The Jahncke house, built in 1896, was one of the first in Audubon Place. [183.3]

ABOVE: St. Charles Avenue, c. 1900. [183.4] BELOW: The renovated carriage house from the 1890 Isidore Newman mansion on Carondelet Street is owned by Robert and Gee Tucker. [183.5]

Neighborhoods Gazetteer

RICE-WILLIAMS HOUSE

1866; Fink Home (1875-1973); renovated 1977–79, Davis Lee Jahncke, Jr., architect
Camp Street, Uptown District

IN 1977 JUDGE AND MRS. DAVID R. M. WILLIAMS purchased and began restoring this raised, center-hall, Italianate villa for their residence. Their spacious lot is part of an entire square that Henry David Rice, an importer and manufacturer, purchased in the Faubourg Delachaise. The Delachaise Plantation was not developed until 1855, five years after it was included in the incorporation of Jefferson City, and it was the last plantation subdivided in the area now known informally as uptown. Rice built the house in 1866, and although the original architect is unknown, it is a fine example of this regional, climatically-suitable type formerly so popular in the suburbs of the city and the surrounding countryside.

In 1875 Rice's divorced wife sold the house and grounds to the City of New Orleans for use as the Fink Home, an asylum for Protestant orphans and widows. It was purchased and established with funds bequeathed to

the city by John David Fink, a German immigrant who made a fortune in real estate. Fink Home served the community for almost a century, finally closing its doors in 1973. Two large rear dormitory wings of brick, erected in 1891, are now detached from the Williams property.

The Williamses converted the asylum into a residence, moving in after a two-year restoration coordinated by architect Davis Lee Jahncke, Jr. Many original exterior and interior features of the house survived its service as an asylum, including a three-story spiral staircase. Gardens, garden walls, fountains, and dependent buildings are new but traditional in character. The Williamses and their architect did the work with great care, and the property is listed on the National Register of Historic Places. Set back from the street, the house commands its handsome grounds, its classical gallery contributing a graceful presence to this old Jefferson City neighborhood.

OPPOSITE: Front elevation. The raised-cottage type originated in the eighteenth century as an accommodation to the subtropical climate and as a precaution against floods. ABOVE: Double parlors with original mantelpieces and ceiling medallions. BELOW RIGHT: Library. Original cast-iron mantelpiece with faux marbre *finish. BELOW LEFT: Side elevation.*

Rice-Williams House

Palacios-Farwell House

1867-68, Henry Howard, architect
St. Charles Avenue, Uptown District, University Section

ABOVE: *Entrance elevation.* BELOW: *Central hallway, with Züber wallpaper installed by the Claiborne family in the 1920s.* RIGHT: *Parlor. Mantelpiece and plasterwork are original.*

In Joan Caldwell's Tulane dissertation, "Italianate Domestic Architecture in New Orleans 1850–1880," she refers to this house as "the most famous example of raised villa architecture in the city." Henry Howard, a distinguished and expressive master of this mid-nineteenth-century transitional style, designed the house in 1867 for Antonio Palacios, a prosperous merchant from Bilbao, Spain.

Palacios had purchased a large corner lot that year facing the New Orleans and Carrollton Railroad. The property was once part of a plantation belonging to New Orleans Mayor Etienne de Boré, who was the first Louisiana planter to successfully granulate sugar on a commercial scale. Cornelius Hurst developed the plantation in 1837, and it became Hurstville, one of the faubourgs incorporated into Jefferson City.

Mr. and Mrs. F. Evans Farwell bought the house in 1953. Architecturally, it combines late Greek Revival and Italianate features in a raised-cottage format, with the standard Anglo-American floor plan, but on a baronial scale. The bisecting central hall is unusually wide and deep and the ceilings are quite high—on the left is a parlor, dining room, and octagonal room; on the right, a library, oval staircase (spiraling from basement to garret), and bedroom. Woodwork and marble mantelpieces are all original.

During the 1920s Charles Claiborne, a descendant of the first American governor of Louisiana, added a dormer in front and installed the French scenic (Züber) wallpaper in the central hall. Otherwise, the house is remarkably intact. Mr. and Mrs. Farwell commented: "There have been very few changes in the house during its 125-year life span, although each of the five families who lived in the house added the modern conveniences of their day: electricity, modern bathrooms, central heat, and air conditioning."

Mr. Farwell's grandfather came to New Orleans from New England in the 1850s to establish a shipping business, and many of the furnishings in the home today are family heirlooms from that era. The Farwells' furnishings are at home here in Henry Howard's classic suburban design.

GOGREVE-BRADBURN-OGDEN HOUSE

1890-91; remodeled 1931, Moise Goldstein, architect
Broadway, Uptown District, Greenville section

Front elevation. This façade dates from 1931 when the house was remodeled, changing the appearance from late-Victorian to Neoclassical.

THE UPTOWN DISTRICT developed as a suburban setting, but it has become urban as the city has expanded. This house originally occupied an entire square, in contrast to the crowded, narrow lots of the Vieux Carré. It is a reminder of many such houses that once stood on entire blocks along Broadway, St. Charles Avenue, and elsewhere in the uptown area.

In 1890 Hermann Gogreve, a prominent German-born businessman and civic leader, purchased square fifty-six of the 1836 suburb plan of Greenville. Gogreve

was the proprietor of a large wholesale grocery firm on Tchoupitoulas Street near Canal Street. His family lived in this house until the 1920s. Dr. and Mrs. William P. Bradburn purchased and subdivided the square in 1931, not to preserve the Gogreve's two-story asymmetrical late-Victorian Italianate house, but to remodel it into the symmetrical Classical Revival temple-form house it is today. Moise Goldstein was their architect; Sam Wilson, Jr., who was then a draftsman in Goldstein's firm, designed some of the elements, and when asked about the style of

Sitting room with a portion of the Ogden Collection.

the remodeling said, "Just eclectic." The floor plan was left much as it had been originally. (The original architect or builder is unknown.)

Preservation arrived in 1978 when Roger Houston Ogden, a New Orleans business and civic leader, purchased the property and began a program of restoring and highlighting architectural and artistic elements as a background for his important art collection. The collection is still being assembled with the help of art historian and specialist in Southern art, Estill Curtis Pennington. "Buck" Pennington's study, *Look Away* (1989) included a number of paintings from the Ogden Collection, among them the luminous example on the dust jacket, *Bayou Plaquemines* (1881) by Joseph Rusling Meeker (1827–1887).

The spacious grounds have also been carefully landscaped as an appropriate setting for the dramatic white-columned house. Ogden has added a swimming pool and fountain, completing a suburban/urban estate that does great credit to the neighborhood.

TOP: *Entrance stair hall. Ogden's extensive collection is rich in nineteenth-century Southern art.* RIGHT: *Living room art gallery.* ABOVE: *Detail of living room. An arrangement of Newcomb pottery under* Bayou Plaquemines, *by Joseph Meeker. The pottery was made at H. Sophie Newcomb College from 1894 until the 1940s.*

Gogreve-Bradburn-Ogden House

BROWN-VILLERE HOUSE
1905, Favrot & Livaudais, architects;
renovated 1987–88, Leonard Salvato, architect
St. Charles Avenue, Uptown District

ST. CHARLES AVENUE from Louisiana Avenue to Napoleon Avenue and beyond narrows slightly, and the oak canopy thickens. Apartments, churches, schools, colleges, and large residences prevail in a post-Civil War mixture of eclectic architectural styles, including Queen Anne, Romanesque Revival, and Richardsonian Romanesque.

The finest residence in the latter rugged, High Victorian medieval style is this majestic house set back and elevated above the avenue. It was built for William Perry Brown, described during his life by the New Orleans *Daily States* as the "bull cotton king."

Henry Hobson Richardson (1838–1886), after his youth in New Orleans and schooling in Boston and Europe, originated the picturesque and romantic style which came to be known as Richardsonian Romanesque during the 1870s. This is Favrot & Livaudais's version a generation later. The 1987–88 renovation for the George Villeres was by Leonard Salvato. Interior design is by Lucile Andrus, whose taste fulfills the French Beaux-Arts quality of the interior. Landscape architecture for the renovation was by René J. L. Fransen.

Favrot & Livaudais altered the normal appearance of the flat New Orleans landscape by building an earth terrace as an elevated base. The normal asymmetry of the

LEFT: Entrance elevation. Terraced above St. Charles Avenue is a grand Richardsonian Romanesque style residence unusual in its symmetry and the refinement of its details. ABOVE: Rear garden and swimming pool. Landscape architecture for the renovation was by René J. L. Fransen.

Brown-Villere House

ABOVE: *Entrance stair hall serves as a sitting room with a Renaissance Revival fireplace. From this great space one enters all chambers of the first floor and ascends to the second.* LEFT: *Entrance foyer. Contemporary primitivism meets Beaux-Arts refinement.* OPPOSITE TOP: *Dining room.* OPPOSITE BOTTOM: *Living room. Inside, the Richardsonian Romanesque house projects a sense of French lightness and Rococo reminiscences.*

Richardsonian style was forsaken for the perfect bilateral symmetry of the entrance façade, which is approached up a broad set of granite steps. The customary massive ruggedness of the style is softened somewhat by a more refined, less ponderous pattern of stonework. The double-pitched tile roof reminds one of colonial Creole plantation houses, which some feel Louisiana-born Richardson himself had in mind with his own characteristically low-pitched roofs.

The turn-of-the-century floor plan is grand, spacious, ceremonial, but open and surprisingly luminous and French, as opposed to the dark oak of the Arts and Crafts

period. Even the stained glass has a light and fanciful French touch.

The Villere family came to Louisiana nine generations ago and has maintained an active and productive presence since then; Jacques Philippe Villere served as governor of Louisiana from 1816 to 1820. Villere ancestors owned plantation land in this area before it was subdivided, and George Villere's grandparents and great-grandparents were frequent guests of William Perry Brown in this very house. How fortunate that George and Frances Villere have restored this stately place, and that they have understood so well how to make a 1905 house their modern home without compromising the integrity of its historical forms and details. How fortunate, too, is St. Charles Avenue that one of its grandest residential landmarks has been so well revived.

BIGELOW COTTAGE
1906; renovated 1948
Audubon Street, Uptown District, University Section

IN THE LATE NINETEENTH CENTURY this section of the uptown area became fashionable as Tulane University and Audubon Park were built. The large, suburban lots were attractive to affluent families, and in 1893 the electrification of the St. Charles Avenue streetcar line made commuting from this neighborhood a standard way of life. The outlying districts were so popular that it was reported in a promotional pamphlet of the day: "Toward them is now tending much of the luxury and wealth of New Orleans."

Not all of the houses built were mansions in scale and opulence. Unknown builders and developers built many bungalows and shotgun cottages using standard plans and stock millwork. A 1915 article in the *Times-Picayune* commented on the "charm of littleness rather than useless piles of gingerbread."

Rather than gingerbread, clearly, the charm of this cottage is Classical, with four Tuscan columns of cypress,

OPPOSITE: *Mary Ferry Bigelow's parents bought this double shotgun in 1926 and converted it into a single-family bungalow in 1948. The Colonial Revival porch is original (1906). ABOVE: Dining room. Ms. Bigelow has lived here her entire life, and displays her interior decorating skills at home with characteristic flair.*

painted white, supporting a pedimented gable. It is one of the earliest houses in the section, one of the few cottages in the immediate area, and was built originally as a double shotgun in the center of two lots. After the first world war, large lots were subdivided and the housing density in the neighborhood increased; this cottage was moved closer to Green Street on a smaller plot.

The present owner's parents purchased the cottage in 1926 when it was still a "double," as they call the type locally.

In 1948 they converted their house to a "single," removing one of the front doors and changing the style of the windows to complement the original Colonial Revival porch.

Mary Ferry Bigelow, an interior decorator, has lived here all of her life. This conveniently located family-home cottage with eleven-foot ceilings, and the "charm of littleness," is a perfect laboratory for her professional practice, well demonstrating the taste and imagination she shares with her friends and clients throughout the city.

Bigelow Cottage

ANDRUS HOUSE
1906; renovated 1947, Myrlin McCullar, architect
Nashville Avenue, Uptown District

THE HURSTVILLE SECTION of the Uptown District, just downriver from Audubon Park, is named for Cornelius Hurst, whose fine plantation house, which was moved to the Orleans Parish line near Metairie in the 1920s, had stood near here. His subdivided property is illustrated on Charles Zimpel's 1834 map, but three years later Hurst lost his fortune in the Panic of 1837. The area which still bears his name grew slowly through the middle years of the century, and for a time was a part of the short-lived Borough of Freeport. By 1894, however, a chamber of commerce pamphlet stated that the Audubon Park area had become a "district of homes—the homes of the thrifty, and even the aristocracy as well." That same year Tulane University was located across St. Charles Avenue from Audubon Park, which had a positive impact on the development of the entire uptown area.

This two-story frame house was built in 1906 and was owned by the same family until 1941. That year Gerald and Lucile Andrus purchased it. Mrs. Andrus is a well-known interior decorator and designer. One of her favorite New Orleans architects was the late Myrlin McCullar, often called "Myrlin the Magician" for the deft sleight of hand with which he tastefully transformed sometimes plain-Jane structures into elegant Classical pavilions, enhancing the plane geometry of their foursquare lines.

In 1947, without "over building" their uptown lot, and without upstaging their street, his wizardry helped Mrs. Andrus change her turn-of-the-century builder's box into a fanlighted Federal style façade with corner pilasters. On the rear they opened up an expanse of wall with large windows and a French door into the garden, where she placed sculpture and terra-cotta pots.

Outside and inside there is the understated artistic sophistication of a much-admired New Orleans decorator's taste, which over a period of a half-century has shaped this formerly undistinguished suburban house into the embodiment of "uptown." Mrs. Andrus says that New Orleanians have a way of picking a neighborhood, making it the center of their lives, and sticking with it for generations. Her renovated house and garden on Nashville Avenue in the Hurstville section contribute to her community a standard of dignified architectural decorum that is a complementary asset to the neighborhood she has called home since 1941.

OPPOSITE TOP: *Front elevation. For the Andrus family, architect McCullar converted a turn-of-the-century suburban box to a restrained, Neoclassical style urban townhouse.* OPPOSITE BOTTOM: *Detail of fireplace wall of living room.* ABOVE: *Entrance stair hall. Mrs. Andrus, a well-known, much-admired interior decorator, often combines contemporary art with European antiques.* LEFT: *Dining room. A portrait of Mr. Andrus is above the fireplace.*

Andrus House

WEIL-CROSBY-LEARY HOUSE

1913, Emile Weil, architect
Audubon Place, Uptown District, University Section

AS ST. CHARLES AVENUE winds its way upriver, festooned with oaks and defined by its timeless streetcar line, it passes between Audubon Park (on the left) and Tulane University (on the right). Just past Tulane is a private, one-street subdivision, Audubon Place. In 1893 Tulane purchased land for its new campus from Judge John Bonner, then sold the upriver edge to George Blackwelder and Company, which developed a single, park-like street "exclusively for the use of the residents." Thirty houses were projected around a landscaped avenue, secluded from St. Charles Avenue by "two stone lodges, joined by an iron arch fifty feet across." The prospectus added: "The park will be completed by the first of October, 1893, by which time it is expected to invite the wealthier element to enter." (*Audubon Place Parade of Homes, 1878,* reprinted 1978.)

After the name Audubon Place was chosen, the street was deeded to a Commission of Property Owners. The Crescent Land and Improvement Company created a subdivision scheme, and houses began to be

OPPOSITE TOP: Entrance loggia. This projecting porch pavilion with cornice and parapet is characteristic of Beaux-Arts design, as is the absolute symmetry. OPPOSITE BOTTOM: Detail of entrance hall looking into the dining room. ABOVE: Entrance stair hall. The delicate staircase is more reminiscent of Colonial French than of the Modern French expressed by the exterior.

constructed; twenty-eight were built by the first decade of the twentieth century. Number Seven, a Shingle-Style house built in 1896, was the home of Paul Jahncke, who served as Secretary-Treasurer of the property owners association during his half-century of residency.

Mr. and Mrs. Prieur J. Leary, Jr., purchased Number Eighteen in 1981 from the Thomas Crosby family, which had moved there after renovating it in 1972. Before that it had been the home of the Herman Weils. Mr. Weil's cousin, Emile Weil, a graduate of the Tulane University School of Architecture, is said to have designed it in 1913. He is best known for banks, theaters, libraries, and mansions designed according to École des Beaux-Arts principles, and in what is often called the Beaux-Arts Classical style. This house is a fine example of one school of that style, sometimes called Modern French. Characteristics are absolute symmetry, columns and arches, advancing and receding planes, projecting pavilions, rich details and materials, and pronounced cornices and parapets. Exterior elevations with these characteristics were supposed to express interior floor plans; and floor plans were always important starting points for an architect trained in Beaux-Arts methods. The resulting design should be a logical and coherent whole, a creative new expression of historical traditions in architecture: thus Modern French Classicism, which Number Eighteen Audubon Place well represents. It is a fine example of the Beaux-Arts style in New Orleans, which more usually leans towards eighteenth-century French and French Creole styles in its search for tradition and classic first principles.

Weil-Crosby-Leary House

Lyons-Milling-Phillips House
1923, Richard Koch, Armstrong & Koch, architect
LaSalle Place, Uptown District, University Section

NEW ORLEANS ARCHITECT Richard Koch (1889–1971) was graduated in 1910 from the first four-year architecture course at Tulane University. It was then that he began the study of Louisiana's historic architecture and gained an appreciation for the importance of measured drawings. His postgraduate studies and apprenticeships took him to Paris and New York, before he returned to New Orleans in 1916 to establish a practice with Charles R. Armstrong. Armstrong & Koch was a pioneer in the restoration and adaptive reuse of buildings of historical and architectural importance.

In addition to restorations and renovations, Koch produced a distinctive body of his own designs in New Orleans and Louisiana. He based these upon his knowledge and appreciation of local and regional types and styles, especially the French and Spanish Creole forms that evolved in Louisiana.

Richard Koch, according to his later partner Sam Wilson, was interested in the Spanish and French Mediterranean background of early New Orleans architecture, as well as in the way the architecture had developed in the New World, evolving in Louisiana to form a Creole vernacular. This uptown house, which he designed in 1920 for Mr. J. Clifford Lyons, is his interpretation of a courtyard- and patio-oriented Mediterranean villa, with influences from the traditional Creole French Quarter house, including French doors and large fanlights. Unlike most suburban houses, it is placed at the street in the Vieux Carré tradition, with a walled patio and the gardens and grounds in the rear.

Mr. and Mrs. Nathaniel P. Phillips, Sr., bought the property from Mrs. Robert Milling in 1955.

OPPOSITE TOP: Front elevation. Entrance directly at the sidewalk in the European urban manner, which also echoes the French Quarter, where the same tradition prevailed. The garden areas are screened from the public, and large, private, outdoor, living spaces are thus provided behind the house. OPPOSITE BOTTOM. Rear view. ABOVE: French doors and fanlights, a Creole feature from Louisiana houses.

Mrs. Phillips, a member of the Garden Study Club of New Orleans (Garden Club of America), concentrated on the gardens and grounds, which had been neglected, and redesigned some of the elements. When Mr. and Mrs. Nathaniel Phillips, Jr., took possession in 1986, they had

Robin Tanner of Tanner Landscape Company again redesign and simplify the scheme, while retaining existing plants and trees. George Hopkins designed a new rear wing, which he unified with the original in the style Koch had devised in 1920.

Lyons-Milling-Phillips House

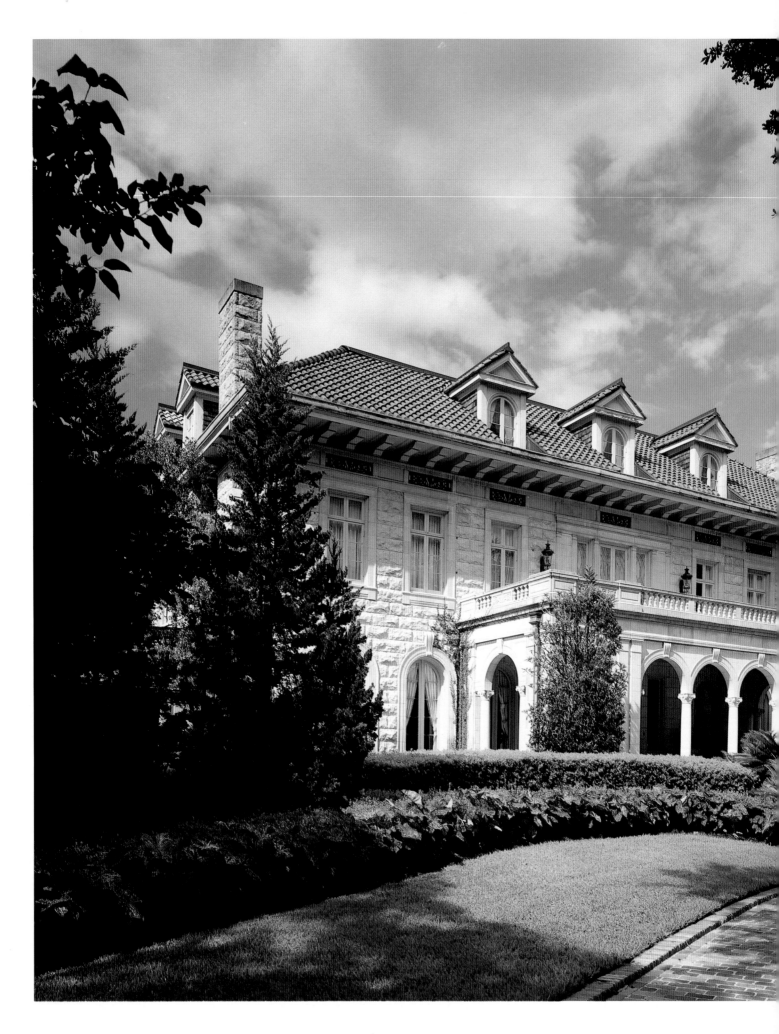

Schlieder-Johnson-Moffett House

1922–23, Favrot & Livaudais, architects;
renovated late-1970s, H. G. Lyons, architect
St. Charles Avenue, Uptown District

St. Charles Avenue extends from Lee Circle to the former town of Carrollton, curving for six miles along an arc roughly parallel to the bend of the river. A leisurely ride on the St. Charles streetcar, itself a National Historic Landmark, will take one past the treasures of the avenue which, sadly, are fewer than once upon a time, but still well worth the slow, but sure, journey. In the Uptown District, near Tulane and Loyola universities and Audubon Park, stands one of the area's opulent residential treasures, an Italian Renaissance Revival, limestone legacy from the early 1920s, the "Schlieder Palace." It was designed by one of the great local firms of that ritzy era, Favrot & Livaudais, for the capitalist Edward G. Schlieder, a "beer baron." His mansion replaced a frame country cottage, embowered among trees and roses, which had stood on the outskirts of Carrollton between State and Palmer streets for many years.

In the late 1970s the mansion was completely renovated and restored over a period of several years by Mr. and Mrs. Norman Johnson; their architect was H. G. Lyons, the landscape architect was René Fransen, and the interior decorator was Thomas R. Collum. The Johnsons added a rear rotunda and an iron-and-marble staircase said to be from the old St. Charles Hotel. In 1984 the mansion became the New Orleans home of Mr. and Mrs. James R. Moffett; their decorator was Rusty Kessenich, ASID.

LEFT: Front elevation facing St. Charles Avenue. In 1923 the house was described as "an edifice of princely splendor."
ABOVE: Loggia porch.

A Superb Home, a pamphlet written when the Schlieder's house was just completed, might have been written about the restored house today: "Fitted with all the appurtenances of the modern American dwelling, it is the opinion of all who have had the pleasure of an inspection . . . that in domestic architecture and appliances for comfort and convenience and . . . exquisite detail and beautiful masonry . . . it has no superior. An edifice of princely splendor, there is no luxury that art, wealth, or desire could suggest that is not to be found there in its most approved and captivating form."

OPPOSITE: *Rear rotunda added in the late 1970s, when the iron-and-marble staircase said to be from the old St. Charles Hotel was installed.* ABOVE: *Dining room.* LEFT: *Front sitting room. The interior decoration, installed in 1984, suggests the opulence of the 1920s when the mansion was built.*

LAK APARTMENT COOPERATIVE

St. Henry Condominium
1923, Moise Goldstein, architect; renovated 1978, Betty L. Moss, architect
St. Charles Avenue, Uptown Historic District, University Section

BY THE MID-1890S St. Charles Avenue had become the Fifth Avenue of New Orleans, a rich mixture of residential, ecclesiastical, and collegiate structures. Numerous stately mansions and institutional buildings lined the street, but sections of the corridor above Jefferson (Peters) Avenue retained a rural appearance—here and there one might see small cottages, gardens, orchards, nurseries, and even farm animals. Some areas of Audubon Park were completely overgrown with wild vegetation. The St. Charles streetcar line in the median was the unifying thread for the long thoroughfare as it curved from the business district to Carrollton.

In the first part of the twentieth century, upper St. Charles became more urbanized as Audubon Park was developed and improved, and numerous apartment buildings were added to the sedate environment.

This four-story design was created by architect Moise Goldstein in 1923 as one of the earliest co-op apartment buildings in New Orleans. It was named the Lak Apartment Cooperative by using the initials of the three resident-owners: Charles Levy, Charles Alltmont, and Solomon H. Kahn. These men had each married one of the Wildenstein sisters of New Orleans, and the three families occupied one floor apiece. The ground floor was used for servants' quarters and a boiler room. Common costs for maintenance, utilities, insurance, and taxes were shared. Within a few years the three couples sold the building to Harry Latter, who lived on one floor and rented the others.

In 1978 Mr. and Mrs. Shepard H. Shushan and two other families purchased the building from Evelyn Lederer Ladd, wife of movie star Alan Ladd, and renovated it for condominium use. Architect Betty L. Moss, a friend of the Shushans, redesigned their third-floor home. The interiors were decorated by Marjorie Shushan and Darryl Schmidt.

Every detail of Goldstein's exterior design was preserved in the meticulous renovation. The stuccoed brick building with a rusticated base and a red tile roof is embellished just as it was when the three Wildenstein sisters lived here. The decorative features are in a Spanish Renaissance motif of

OPPOSITE: Front elevation. Facing St. Charles Avenue, this condominium apartment building is part of the architectural mixture along one of the city's most sophisticated boulevards. ABOVE: Dining room. Above St. Charles Avenue, a chic and stylish condominium that might be in Paris or New York.

cast concrete and wrought iron, including arched openings, recessed and overhanging balconies, balustrades, and cornices and surrounds ornamented with relief sculpture. The entrance on the avenue is fronted by balustraded garden terraces, and a metal marquee shelters the side door. From the balconies, the co-op units look out on the oaks of St. Charles Avenue at Henry Clay Street. This intersection of streets provided the inspiration for renovating the Lak even further by combining their names—it is now called the St. Henry Condominium.

DREYFOUS-PAINE HOUSE

1928, F. Julius Dreyfous, architect; renovated 1970, Myrlin McCullar, architect
Audubon Street, Uptown District, University Section

OPPOSITE: Front elevation. Designed by an architect as his own residence in the style of Age-of-Reason France, it is urban and suburban at one and the same time. ABOVE: Entrance stair hall.

JULIUS DREYFOUS, of the architectural firm of Weiss, Dreyfous, & Seiferth, built this, his own home, in the style of eighteenth-century France. Rather than Creole French, it is in the more aristocratic taste of king and court, a townhouse pavilion of the sort one might find in Paris or Versailles. It is an expression from the first decades of the twentieth century of the sophisticated eclecticism of American architects, many of whom had trained in France or at least in the École des Beaux-Arts tradition at architecture schools in America. This did not mean architects of that era designed only in French style; rather, it was an analytical technique, an academic eclecticism, used in the design of traditional-style buildings such as this house. For example, his firm designed a home

nearby, Number Twenty-seven Audubon Place, a residence in the Spanish Colonial Revival style.

In 1970 Dr. and Mrs. Lincoln Paine renovated the property as their home. Their architect was Myrlin McCullar, whose subtle eclecticism continued the aesthetic techniques of Dreyfous's era, especially in the garden, where McCullar designed an overall formal scheme in conjunction with landscape architect Dorothy Hardie. This included redesigning the guest house to match the style of the main building. A number of other designers helped the Paines, among them Lucile Andrus, one of uptown's favorite interior decorators, whose classic taste perfectly matched the suave architecture of Dreyfous and McCullar.

ABOVE: Living room. The interiors were decorated by Lucile Andrus to complement the architecture. OPPOSITE TOP: Rear elevation and formal grounds. OPPOSITE BOTTOM: Servants' quarters and parterre garden.

Dreyfous-Paine House

ABOVE: *The Carrollton Railroad Station, designed by James Gallier, Jr., was built in 1851. [214.1] BELOW: The Carrollton Courthouse, built in 1855, later served as a public school. [214.2]*

BELOW: *This c. 1890 shotgun cottage is the home of Mr. and Mrs. Ellis Marsalis, Jr., the city's "first family of jazz." [214.3]*

Carrollton District

Carrollton is the most upriver faubourg within the New Orleans city limits, about six miles from the Vieux Carré by way of St. Charles Avenue. In the early nineteenth century, the McCarty family owned a plantation in Jefferson Parish that was once a part of the great Bienville grant, and in 1830 they sold it to a group of investors intent on creating a resort out from town on the river. In 1833 Charles F. Zimpel, a German engineer and surveyor, drew the plans for subdivision, and in the following two years coordinated the development of the New Orleans and Carrollton Railroad, a crucial part of the venture. Named for an American, General William Carroll, who camped here with his Kentuckians in 1815 just before the Battle of New Orleans, the town became a popular resort with a fine hotel; in 1845 it was incorporated and in 1852 became the seat of Jefferson Parish. Carrollton was annexed to New Orleans in 1874 as the Seventh District, so the Jefferson Parish seat was moved to Gretna across the river, and the Orleans Parish boundary was moved up to its current location at Monticello Street.

By the Civil War the town had a population of 1,693, but afterward it began to grow rapidly as many former slaves left plantations and moved to the New Orleans area. Many found work on Carrollton's dairy and vegetable farms. Near the river is an African-American neighborhood that began to grow after the war and is known as the Black Pearl. Carrollton's growth slowed again until 1893, when the introduction of electric streetcars on the St. Charles line made Canal Street more easily accessible.

The evidence of a turn-of-the-century building surge is abundant, but an earlier suburban ambience is still implied among the shaded avenues, and there remain a number of antebellum houses. One of the most remarkable is the Nathaniel Newton Wilkinson house, on South Carrollton Avenue, a Tudor Gothic Revival villa built in 1849–50. Set on spacious grounds, it is one of only a handful of houses in New Orleans in that picturesque style. Carrollton also contains an exceptionally large selection (more than 1,350) of New Orleans shotgun houses—some of the finest examples of that sometimes plain and humble style. These ornate shotguns are a hallmark of Carrollton.

A major landmark within the district is the Greek Revival Carrollton Courthouse (1855), 719 Carrollton Avenue, designed by Henry Howard. Although it was erected as the Jefferson Parish Courthouse, it has functioned as a public school since the town was annexed in 1874. The Carrollton Historic District was listed on the National Register in 1987.

WILKINSON-COE HOUSE

1849–50; restored 1965, Koch & Wilson, architects
South Carrollton Avenue, Carrollton Historic District

Front elevation. This is one of the few Gothic Revival style houses in the city, but this superb example is one of the best in the United States.

ALTHOUGH THE GOTHIC REVIVAL was sometimes the style of choice for churches and government buildings in the antebellum South, it was seldom used for residential architecture. When this romantic style was chosen, it was most likely for a rural estate or in a resort setting such as the village of Carrollton, laid out upriver from New Orleans in 1833. This Carrollton villa was built in 1849–50 for Nathaniel Newton Wilkinson, an officer in the New Orleans Canal and Banking Company, which developed the resort village. The architect is unknown, but the villa is a good example of a style fashionable in the mid-nineteenth century in architectural pattern books that illustrated various types of house plans and elevations. Such books became quite popular, especially for the design of rural residences, and Wilkinson's Gothic villa closely resembles designs in William H. Ranlett's *The Architect*, published in New York in 1847.

Cruciform in plan, the two-story brick house with Tudor chimneys was originally plastered and scored to resemble stone, but the plaster has since been removed. Decorative details include Gothic finials,

bargeboards, and balconies with trefoil designs. The unusual windows are double-hung but designed to imitate the small, diagonal-paned casement windows of the Tudor Period.

The house was damaged in 1965 by Hurricane Betsy, and the present owners, Dr. and Mrs. A. Jason Coe, hired the firm of Koch & Wilson, Architects, to supervise restoration repairs with their usual scholarly care. Dr. Coe values "the beautiful Gothic cove moldings and medallions, the circular staircase, and Gothic detailing throughout." He adds "the overgrown yard gives a country feel on now busy Carrollton Avenue."

The villa faces Carrollton Avenue, and is not far from the site of the old depot and hotel that served the New Orleans and Carrollton Railroad. Designed by James Gallier, Jr., and John Turpin in 1851, the year af-

OPPOSITE: Entrance stair hall. The Gothic Revival staircase is rare in New Orleans. ABOVE: Dining room. RIGHT: Parlor. The owners respect the original 1850 architectural details and have furnished this room compatibly.

ter Mr. Wilkinson's home was completed, the Gothic Revival depot with its crenelated towers must have presented a charming welcome to tourists arriving at the village. The Wilkinson-Coe house, originally the centerpiece of an entire block and today still nestled in a large garden with live oaks and lush exotic plantings, is a reminder of the architecture and setting of those rural resort days in Carrollton.

Wilkinson-Coe House

Holy Cross High School in 1899. [218.1]

ABOVE: The Lombard Plantation house, built in 1826, from a photograph taken in the 1930s. [218.2] BELOW: Early houses along Levee Road in the district now called Bywater. [218.3]

Bywater and Holy Cross Districts

The historic districts of Bywater and Holy Cross are downriver from the first Creole faubourg, Marigny, and were relatively slow-developing areas of New Orleans. Bywater is just that, nestled along the low levee of the Mississippi on the lands of former plantations and the subdivided faubourgs of Daunois, Montegut, Clouet (where the architect Benjamin Henry Latrobe owned a house during his New Orleans sojourn), Montreuil, Carraby, and Lesseps. Holy Cross District, named after a Catholic boys' school in the area, extends along the river to the St. Bernard Parish boundary.

The region downriver from Marigny was for many years known as the Ninth Ward, a huge political ward covering the eastern part of the parish, which, until well into the twentieth century, was mostly swampland. Along the river, plantations were subdivided during the first half of the nineteenth century, but the area, prone to frequent flooding, grew slowly. The natural levee along this part of the river is narrow, extending back only a few blocks, and development was limited until the introduction of mechanical drainage after 1900.

Today in Bywater a lone reminder of the plantation era, the Lombard manor house, stands hidden among later structures at 3933 Chartres Street. A small-scale early nineteenth-century version of a French colonial plantation house, it was built in 1826 by Joseph Lombard, Sr., for his son. Elevated on a high basement, this Creole manor has an open gallery facing the river and an enclosed gallery with *cabinets* in the rear. When it was built, there was a wide view over the Mississippi levee. Only a few years after its construction, the plantation was sold and developed as part of the Faubourg Carraby, but the main house and its appurtenances survived as a small estate for several decades.

Bywater was mainly a working-class neighborhood, with modest wooden cottages predominating. Similar to the adjacent Marigny district, its population was a mixture of Creoles and free people of color, joined by new immigrants from Germany, Ireland, and Italy. The earliest houses are of the type now called Creole cottages, of which there are quite a number, intermixed with a multitude of single and double shotgun cottages exuberantly embellished with Victorian gingerbread. Riverfront houses have been demolished or moved because of levee setbacks, and small industrial intrusions have altered its residential character, but the area retains a distinctly nineteenth-century atmosphere. The Bywater District, which was named for a local telephone exchange, was entered into the National Register in 1986, and there is an active

Bywater Neighborhood Association whose emblem is the World War I memorial arch in Macarty Square.

Further downriver expansion was impeded by the location of the Ursuline Convent (1826–1912), and, when it was moved, by the construction of the Industrial Canal. As a result, the area now known as the Holy Cross District grew even more slowly than adjacent Bywater. At the end of the nineteenth century, almost all of the development was scattered within a few blocks of the river. This is the most easterly historic district of Orleans Parish and it consists of a grid of about sixty blocks, mainly residential and similar to Bywater, although lots are larger and the blocks are somewhat less filled in.

Holy Cross contains about 635 structures ranging in type from Creole to Bungalow. The Italianate style was popular in the district, as it was in other parts of the city. The landmark Doullut houses were built in 1905 and 1913 by steamboat captain Milton P. Doullut and his son Paul near the river not far from the Industrial Canal and about a mile from the Orleans Parish line. These intriguing raised cottages are eclectic indeed, with influences from Japanese and steamboat architecture, topped by green glazed tile roofs and pilothouse cupolas (as though Mark Twain's steamboat had run aground in Tokyo Bay). The object of many pilgrimages to the neighborhood, these unique Doullut twins are among the most notable houses in the entire city.

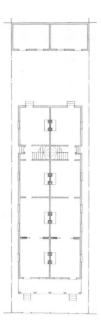

The house style that many New Orleanians most associate with their city is the shotgun. The basic plan is a narrow layout with all rooms in a straight line and usually with no hall. The doors between rooms are often in a row, so that a shot fired through the front door would go through them all. The variations on the basic, or "single," plan are the "double" (a duplex) and the "camelback," (left) where a second story is built over the back rooms. Side hall and side gallery versions also exist. Embellishments vary according to era and location. The shotgun house first appeared in New Orleans in the 1830s, and from the Civil War until about 1900 the plan was the staple of working-class housing. [219.1]

Louisa Street in the Bywater District illustrates many of the variations of cottage types so prevalent in New Orleans. These paintings by New Orleans artist James Blanchard show several varieties of shotgun and Creole cottage types. At the far left above is a double shotgun. [219.2] Below from left to right are two Creole cottages, a double camelback, and two doubles. [219.3]

Andre Trevigne has transformed an old bank building on Dauphine Street into a distinctive home. [219.4]

Neighborhoods Gazetteer

LEWIS-POCHÉ COTTAGE

Early nineteenth century with mid-nineteenth-century additions
Clouet Street, Bywater District

THE WELL-KNOWN ARCHITECT Benjamin Henry Latrobe purchased a house in the Faubourg Clouet in 1819, about a mile below the Place d'Armes (Jackson Square) on Levee Street at the upper corner of Clouet Street facing the Mississippi River. Mrs. Latrobe described it as "a very excellent and convenient dwelling, buried in Orange, Pomegranate, Oleander, and Althea trees, . . ." in a neighborhood ". . . made up of a range of residences . . . ornamented in a variety of tastes."

The Latrobes' house was lost long ago, but Mrs. Latrobe might have been describing Paul Poché's home today, charmingly "buried" by large shrubs of various kinds, among them crape myrtles, one of the city's favorite old plants. The house is a frame, hipped-roof Creole cottage raised on low brick piers, updated with Doric box columns and other Classical Revival features. It is a five bay, one-and-a-half-story house, galleried, with a Creole plan (hall-less), and set back on the lot beyond a low fence.

The house may date from the early years of Faubourg Clouet, which was subdivided in 1807 and again in 1809 by surveyor Barthélémy Lafon for Brognier de Clouet. Research indicates the original owner might have been Judge Joshua Lewis, a district court judge appointed by

OPPOSITE: Front elevation. A five-bay Creole cottage updated with Classical Revival features and restored as his home in the Bywater District by Elmore Paul Poché, Jr. ABOVE: Living room detail. Bizarre Bazaar might be an appropriate description of the Poché style.

Lewis-Poché Cottage

LEFT and BELOW: Dining room. "Interior styled by owner," Poché wrote. He added: "The house is decorated with numerous paper leaves and flowers, vivid objects designed and built by Poché for the floats of the Mistick Krewe of Comus."

President Jefferson at the time of the Louisiana Purchase in 1803. The early records are confusing, but it is known that Judge Lewis's son, John L. Lewis, who held office as Orleans Parish sheriff, state senator, and then mayor of New Orleans, owned the house until 1845.

Although the house is relatively small, the grounds were once extensive, with a two-story brick stable and carriage house, a two-story brick kitchen and servants' quarters in the rear, and a geometric parterre garden which occupied an entire lot adjacent to the house. All of these have disappeared over time, and Paul Poché describes the grounds today as: "Late-Creole, Jungle-style, with birds."

Of his decor, Poché wrote for *Classic New Orleans*: "The house is decorated with numerous paper leaves and flowers, vivid objects designed and built by Poché for the floats of The Mistick Krewe of Comus. Chromolithographed carnival parade bulletins and gilded invitations abound evoking year round the gay spirits of Mardi Gras past and future. There are a multitude of *objets d'art* and *trouvé* combined in a unique and interesting manner to create a very evocative and personal decor." The artist's own words are far too original and apt to be improved; they characterize exactly and creatively one of the truly "unique and interesting" homes in New Orleans.

Lewis-Poché Cottage

HELMKE-COOPER HOUSE

1885

Chartres Street, Bywater District

IN 1885 BERNHARDT WILLIAM HELMKE built this raised, center-hall house on Levee Street facing the Mississippi River, but twenty years later when the levee was changed, he had to move it farther from the river to its present site on Chartres Street. The house has been altered little since it was home for Mr. Helmke, a sugar boiler who probably worked at one of the large sugar refineries downriver from the city.

Vintage is the keynote of this house, inside and out: the kitchen and main bathroom have period plumbing fixtures; there is a functioning nineteenth-century, groundwater well in the front yard; and a cypress cistern of the kind that was once ubiquitous in New Orleans is in the back yard. The furnishings are old and interesting, among them a c. 1820 Louisiana piece, a child's armoire of cherry and poplar, with beehive feet.

The architecture is certainly vintage—Italianate in style, late Classical Revival, almost *retardataire* for the 1880s. A type of the popular raised villa, it echoes the

form of its next-door neighbor at 3933 Chartres, the landmark Joseph Lombard house, a Creole plantation manor house built in 1826. Although built a half-century apart, these houses share the traditional exterior configuration of a vernacular form that originated in the colonial period, with brick piers and hipped roof extending over a front gallery. Both houses seem earlier than they are: they were "old-fashioned" even when they were built. (Vintage: of old, recognized, and enduring interest, importance, or quality: classic; old-fashioned.)

The current owners of the Helmke house are Marc and Mary Cooper, active preservationists who have renovated three houses in the Bywater District. Marc Cooper is a renovation carpenter and was the founding president of the Bywater Neighborhood Association. Mary Cooper is the "resident horticulturalist" and has developed a water garden, an herb garden, and planted fruit trees. Their grounds now contain many native and naturalized species as well as a variety of semitropicals.

OPPOSITE: Front elevation. A late example of colonial architecture as interpreted in Italianate, Classical Revival terms, with a central entrance and center-hall plan. Raised on a high basement, it sits near the levee in Bywater. ABOVE: Rear elevation. Cypress cisterns were a regular feature of houses in the city for more than a century. This is a rare survivor. TOP: Double parlors. The house is furnished simply, with a Creole flavor. LEFT: A c.1820 Louisiana armoire for a child.

Helmke-Cooper House

Algiers Point District

As the Mississippi meanders toward the Gulf of Mexico, its principal direction is from north to south, but in southern Louisiana the river makes a gradual swing to the east, and New Orleans, though technically on the east bank, is actually north of the river. In the nineteenth century this was often referred to as the left bank (obviously from the perspective of downriver travel). Almost directly across the river from the Vieux Carré is Algiers Point, the site of earliest development on the right, or west, bank. Algiers Point is part of the larger Algiers, which extends about twelve miles downriver.

John Law's Company of the Indies owned the area on

ABOVE: DuVerje plantation house. [226.1] BELOW: This double shotgun cottage, constructed in 1892, was featured on the Public Broadcasting System television series, "This Old House," in 1991 when it was converted into a single house for Elvis and Jean Golden. [226.2]

the west bank until it was returned to the French government in 1732. The French ceded the area to Spain in 1762, and in 1769 the Spanish began dividing the land for private cultivation. In 1805 the area was included in Orleans Parish, but, except for the early settlement at the point, it remained sparsely settled plantation land until the latter half of the nineteenth century. It was known by various names until 1840, when the title Algiers first appeared in the City Directory. The neighborhood called Algiers Point had been previously named Duverjeville, or sometimes Duverjeburg, after the DuVerjes, who had a plantation there.

The Canal Street Ferry began operating between New Orleans and the west bank in 1827, and still provides an important transportation link. Because of the ferry and the evolving shipbuilding and dry-dock industries, Algiers began to grow in the 1840s and 1850s. It became a terminus for the Morgan Railroad in 1856, and when Southern Pacific acquired the line, the facilities were improved and expanded. Rail connection to the east bank was accomplished by massive ferries, the largest of which was the *Mastodon*. In 1870 Algiers was annexed by New Orleans as the Fifth District, but retained its own jurisdiction and city and criminal courts. The courthouse was the old DuVerje plantation house, built in 1812.

In 1895 a tragic fire consumed about 200 buildings, including the courthouse, which was rebuilt in 1896 in a turreted, Italianate style on the same spot at 225 Morgan Street, where it stands today as the Second City Court and Community Center. The earliest houses had been in the Greek Revival style, and many of these were destroyed in the 1895 fire, but several two-story survivors can be found near the levee, along Delaronde, Lavergne, Pelican, and Vallette streets. Houses on Algiers Point, however, are predominately one-story Victorian shotgun cottages, many in rows. Small and neat front gardens are a familiar sight, and resemble those in the Irish Channel District. Corner stores are often two-story with a cast-iron gallery over the *banquette*. Oak-lined Opelousas Avenue has shops and restaurants. Of the four churches that are primary landmarks, the Country Gothic Mt. Olivet, dating from the mid-1850s, is the oldest.

This quaint neighborhood was designated a National Register district in 1978, and community renovation is being encouraged by the Algiers Point Association and the Preservation Resource Center through its Operation Comeback. The small-town atmosphere of Algiers Point is quite a contrast to the skyscrapers looming across the river in the heart of modern New Orleans, but it is still only a short ferry ride away.

The rooftops of Central City from St. Charles Avenue at St. Mary Street, c. 1922. The spire of St. John the Baptist Church rises above the surrounding buildings at the far left. The skyline of the Central Business District is in the distance. [227.1]

Central City District

This neighborhood is "back of town," just on the north side of St. Charles Avenue from the Garden and Lower Garden districts. The southern portion of Central City was subdivided about the same time as the Lower Garden District, but the area grew slowly because of its wet, low terrain. The neighborhood north of Carondelet was developed in the 1840s and 1850s apparently for Irish immigrants working nearby, but there was virtually no development beyond South Claiborne Avenue upriver from the canal until the modern drainage system was installed in the early twentieth century.

Most dwellings in the area, particularly in the northern reaches, are one-story wood-frame residences, built close to the sidewalk—standard shotgun and double shotgun houses rented to workers. There are some camelback shotguns as well. Nearer St. Charles Avenue there were once a few country villas, but they are now gone. A few antebellum mansions remain, and in this area there are more two-story houses and other buildings with architectural decoration. Throughout the Central City District, buildings are usually ornamented only on their façades. There are stylistic variations: Greek Revival, Italianate,

and Queen Anne, but the buildings are basically consistent in form, type, and scale. Freret Row in the 1700 block of Second Street illustrates this. It is a row of five almost identical detached houses designed by the architect William Alfred Freret and erected by the Freret family in 1860. The two-story, double-galleried houses combine elements of Greek Revival and Italianate styles, a New Orleans type found throughout older parts of the city.

In late-nineteenth-century New Orleans, people of different races and cultural backgrounds often lived as neighbors, and this was certainly true in the working-class suburbs now known as Central City. More recently it became an important African-American neighborhood. In the late nineteenth and early twentieth centuries it was the home of the great Buddy Bolden, whose jazz band is considered by many music historians to be the original.

Central City was placed on the National Register in 1982. One of the most significant architectural landmarks within its boundaries is the Church of St. John the Baptist (1869–70), designed by Albert Diettel. Its baroque gold dome rises 125 feet, towering over the surrounding neighborhood, enhancing the skyline above Dryades Street.

Gentilly is a twentieth-century suburb northeast of the Vieux Carré at Lake Pontchartrain. This is the Gentilly home of Mr. and Mrs. Norman C. Francis. Mr. Francis is president of Xavier University.

Other Neighborhoods

The designated historic districts and their various neighborhoods, as chronicled above, include the urban area of New Orleans essentially as it existed about 1900, but there are other neighborhoods outside these districts which are important to the history of the city and its more recent architectural development.

Another "back-of-town" neighborhood is Midcity, which stretches from Claiborne Avenue to the Metairie Ridge (City Park Avenue) between the Esplanade Ridge and the Pontchartrain Expressway. Heavy residential growth reached Broad Street by the mid-1870s, but the threat of floods inhibited further development until the drainage system was installed.

When the backswamp areas were drained in the early decades of the twentieth century, growth toward Lake Pontchartrain accelerated, and land south of the Metairie and Gentilly ridges was rapidly developed. The area north of the two ridges, unprotected from the wind-driven waters of the lake, was much more susceptible to flooding and thus a higher risk. There were nineteenth-century lakefront amusement parks with adjunct communities but only a few subdivisions until the completion of the lake seawall in the early 1930s. Growth remained modest until after World War II, when the area finally began to flourish, and by the late 1950s, urban New Orleans had reached Lake Pontchartrain.

The Gentilly region, originally composed of farms and plantations along the ridge and Gentilly Road (now Gentilly Boulevard), was still relatively open during the 1930s. It is known for its nurseries, the grounds of the Parks and Parkways Commission, and the handsome Georgian Revival buildings constructed in 1935 at Dillard University. On the west side of City Park, south of the Lakeview neighborhood, are several large cemeteries as well as the New Orleans Country Club. Between these and Old Metairie (in Jefferson Parish) is Country Club Gardens, a small, somewhat isolated subdivision of only a few tree-lined streets established in 1924. Several fine examples of mid-twentieth-century domestic architecture are located there, including splendid Longue Vue.

PRESIDENT'S HOME, DILLARD UNIVERSITY

1936, Moise Goldstein, architect
2601 Gentilly Boulevard
Gentilly

DILLARD UNIVERSITY opened at its present forty-eight-acre site in the Gentilly section of New Orleans in September 1935. (Gentilly is named for a French plantation that occupied the high natural levees along Bayou Sauvage, also called Bayou Gentilly.)

The history of Dillard dates back to two small schools established in 1869 for the education of African-Americans in the post-war period. These schools eventually became Straight College and New Orleans University, and in 1930 they merged to form Dillard University, named for James Hardy Dillard, whose distinguished service in black education in the South well qualified him for the honor.

The campus architect was Moise Goldstein, F.A.I.A., one of the founders of the School of Architecture at Tulane University. The landscape architect was William S. Wiedorn, who helped design City Park. Since 1972 architect Milton G. Scheuermann, Jr., a former associate of

the Goldstein firm who began designing campus buildings in the 1950s, has been the Dillard University architect. That year he made minor renovations to the president's home, which was built in 1936 in the Georgian Revival style of Goldstein's original campus buildings. Dillard's first president, Dr. William Stuart Nelson, occupied the house between 1937 and 1940.

Dr. and Mrs. Samuel DuBois Cook have resided in the house since 1975, when Dr. Cook became president of the university. Both of the Cooks are natives of Georgia and were graduated from distinguished black colleges in the Atlanta University Center. In this modified Georgian Revival presidential mansion, the Cooks have entertained former President Gerald Ford, Mrs. Coretta Scott King, Dr. Benjamin E. Mays, and the Rev. Jesse Jackson, among other notable guests. Large university receptions for events such as Founders' Day, are held in the garden, which features a fish pond and is shaded by a green canopy of oaks.

Opposite: Stair hall. African Birth, *by Dr. Willie F. Hooker, is symbolic of the new emerging Africa. Above: Garden elevation. Large university receptions are held here. Below: Living room with view of the garden room.* A Nigerian Village, *by Jane Obiago, hangs above the sofa, and complements the African accoutrements.*

LONGUE VUE HOUSE AND GARDEN
1939–42, William and Geoffrey Platt, architects, Ellen Biddle Shipman, landscape architect
7 Bamboo Road

ABOVE: *Main façade, west elevation. The great avenue of live oaks leading up to the Palladian entrance was planted in 1940.* OPPOSITE: *South elevation. The Spanish Court garden dates from the mid-1960s. Designed for Mrs. Stern by William Platt, architect of the house, it is on axis with the drawing room and Palladian portico.*

THIS EIGHT-ACRE, SEMI-URBAN, SEMI-SUBURBAN ESTATE spreads out adjacent to the Orleans Parish line, the New Orleans Country Club golf course, and the Seventeenth Street Canal. It is the farthest upriver property in *Classic New Orleans*. ("Old Metairie" is just across the Jefferson Parish line.) The Longue Vue Foundation was created by the extraordinarily philanthropic Edgar Bloom Stern family, which made Longue Vue its home for fifty years. The family serves as trustee for the private museum, which is open for the public's benefit. (The gardens were opened in 1968 and the entire tract in 1980.) Edith Rosenwald Stern (1895–1980) made this her primary residence until 1978. Her husband, Edgar B. Stern, a cotton broker associated with his family's firm, died in 1959; he was one of the city's most respected and public-spirited citizens. Mrs. Stern's father was Julius Rosenwald, one of the founders and principal stockholders of Sears, Roebuck & Company.

The Sterns began acquiring this land soon after their marriage in 1921. On a smaller portion, they built the

first Longue Vue in 1923. They gradually acquired additional acreage, and in 1935 Mrs. Stern engaged Ellen Biddle Shipman (1870–1950), the dean of women landscape architects, to lay out the outlines of the garden acreage still evident today. The Sterns referred to Miss Shipman as Lady Ellen, and considered her the godmother of Longue Vue; in time she would help with many aspects, including interior decoration.

Lady Ellen's landscape scheme created a desire for a house specifically related to the new grounds, gardens, and vistas. After the Sterns engaged architects to accomplish that, they moved their first house to the nearby corner of Metairie Road and Garden Lane, where it is still a private residence.

Ellen Shipman introduced the Sterns to the eminent architect William Platt, F.A.I.A. (1897–1984) who, with his brother Geoffrey (1905–1985), began work in 1939 to create the present house in the Classical Revival style, sited perfectly in its existing landscape setting. The Platts' father, Charles Adams Platt (1861–1933), who had

Longue Vue House and Garden

RIGHT: Drawing room. The largest, most formal room, with ceilings of fourteen-and-a-half feet. Federal style, pine mill-work was designed around an antique Philadelphia mantelpiece with Robert Wellford details memorializing George Washington. BELOW: Hall detail, looking into drawing room. FOLLOWING PAGE: The upper reception and stair hall. The spiral stairway extends three stories; classically inspired circular spaces are used throughout this semi-urban, semi-suburban Southern American country house.

taught Miss Shipman, was a leader in the design of American country houses. That movement espouses, as one of its primary themes, the relation of houses to their gardens and the terrain, in the manner of classical villas.

The Sterns admired the classical architecture of Louisiana. They took the Platt brothers to visit landmarks such as Shadows-on-the-Teche, on which the east elevation of Longue Vue is based; and the pedimented, raised-cottage Beauregard-Keyes house in the Vieux Carré, which provided inspiration for the south and west elevations. From the west, the house is approached through a courtyard and live oak alley leading towards a symmetrical five-part format with a main block and flanking pavilions linked by colonnades; this five-part plan reflects the primary and continuing influence of

Andrea Palladio's sixteenth-century Renaissance Classicism. The Platts' Palladian villa realizes the Sterns' desire for a house and garden that interact; each room incorporating a magnificent view as formal, axial, sight lines are basic to the entire conception.

One large garden is surrounded by six smaller ones, each different in color and design. The Spanish Court,

or South Lawn, dating from 1965–66, is the largest and most formal. Mrs. Stern, who was interested in Louisiana's Spanish heritage, visited the fourteenth-century Generalife Gardens of the Alhambra in Granada, Spain. She asked William Platt to create a Moorish-Spanish design with fountains, *jardiniere* planting, and mosaic walks. This provides a dramatic perspective from

the formal drawing room on the principal floor.

Mrs. Stern was a member, and at one time president, of the Garden Study Club of New Orleans, an affiliate of the Garden Club of America. Longue Vue House and Garden as a home, as a thing of beauty, and as an educational institution embodies the vision of two remarkable civic leaders.

EPILOGUE

Classic New Orleans is about the place known to caring residents; a book written for them and for visitors who would also know its secrets. This is a book for the true aficionado-resident and for a visitor-tourist who might be persuaded to join in the fun fray of the magic eccentricities of the present and past of New Orleans.

To challenge its past will certainly take resourceful and imaginative future generations. For them and for us we have gathered as much of classic New Orleans into this one volume as we could, as much as has survived over time. The gauntlet is laid down. A city is almost always a damsel in distress; it is we and our descendants who must save her again and again.

SELECTED BIBLIOGRAPHY

New Orleans itself was the most primary source: its buildings, architecture, parks, gardens, streets, neighborhoods, districts, and visible traditions. The seven-volume Friends of the Cabildo survey series *New Orleans Architecture,* begun in 1971, was another fundamental source. Issues of *Preservation in Print,* the newspaper/newsletter of the New Orleans Preservation Resource Center (PRC), had invaluable articles on the neighborhoods, districts, landmarks, and architecture of the city; the entire run of these should be considered part of this bibliography. Samuel Wilson, Jr., his writings and commentaries, was a basic source. National Register of Historic Places nomination forms for New Orleans properties were basic sources for individual buildings, as well as historic districts. The data sheets, produced by property owners at the author's request, which are filed at the PRC, were helpful in the articles on individual homes. Paul St. Martin III, his knowledge, insights, personal library, friends, and connections, made the manuscript a better document. Others who provided fundamental knowledge of the city, many of them members of the PRC *Classic New Orleans* book committee, are listed in the acknowledgments.

A Century of Architecture in New Orleans, 1857–1957. New Orleans: American Institute of Architects, New Orleans Chapter, 1957.

A Guide to New Orleans Architecture. New Orleans: American Institute of Architects, New Orleans Chapter, 1974.

A Superb Home, Residence of Edward G. Schlieder. New Orleans: Private printing, 1924.

Audubon Place Parade of Homes, December 17, 1878. New Orleans: Preservation Resource Center, 1978.

Barbour, Andrew and Jacqueline Russell, eds. *Fodor's 91, New Orleans.* New York: Fodor's Travel Publications, Inc., 1991.

Baumbach, Richard O., Jr., and William E. Borah. *The Second Battle of New Orleans, "A History of the Vieux Carré Riverfront-Expressway Controversy."* Tuscaloosa: The University of Alabama Press, 1981.

Cable, George Washington. *Old Creole Days.* New York: The Heritage Press, 1943.

Cable, Mary. *Lost New Orleans.* New York: American Legacy Press, 1984.

Caldwell, Joan G. "Italianate Domestic Architecture in New Orleans 1850-1880." Ph.D dissertation, Tulane University, 1975 (Ann Arbor, Mich.: University Microfilms, 1975).

Carter, Hodding. *John Law Wasn't So Wrong.* Baton Rouge: Esso Standard Oil Company, 1952.

Castellanos, Henry C. *New Orleans As It Was.* New Orleans: L. Graham Co., Ltd., Publisher, 1895.

Chase, John C. *Frenchman, Desire, Good Children, and Other Streets of New Orleans.* New Orleans: Robert L. Crager & Company, 1949.

Christovich, Mary Louise, et al, eds. *New Orleans Architecture.* 7 vols. Gretna, La.: Pelican Publishing Co., 1971–1989.

Christovich, Mary Louise. *New Orleans Interiors.* New Orleans: Friends of the Cabildo, 1980.

Costa, Louis, et al. *Streetcar Guide to Uptown New Orleans.* New Orleans: Transi Tour, Inc., 1980.

Cullison, William R. III. *Architecture in Louisiana, A Documentary History.* New Orleans: Tulane University, Southeastern Architectural Archive, 1983.

Curtis, Nathaniel Cortlandt. *New Orleans, Its Old Houses, Shops and Public Buildings.* Philadelphia: 1933.

Edwards, Jay D. *Louisiana's Remarkable French Vernacular Architecture.* Baton Rouge: Department of Geography and Anthropology, Louisiana State University, 1988.

Filson, Dean Ronald C., ed. *The New Orleans Guide.* London: International Architect Publishing, Ltd., 1984.

Fitch, James Marston. "Creole Architecture 1718–1860: The Rise and Fall of a Great Tradition." In *The Past as Prelude.* New Orleans: Tulane University, 1968.

Gallier, James. *Autobiography.* New York: Da Capo, 1973.

Garvey, Joan B. and Mary Lou Widmer. *Beautiful Crescent, A History of New Orleans.* New Orleans: Garner Press, Inc., 1982.

Gorin, Abbye A. *Conversations with Samuel Wilson, Jr., "Dean of Architectural Preservation in New Orleans."* New Orleans: Louisiana Landmarks Society, 1991.

Gosner, Pamela. *Caribbean Georgian.* Washington, D. C.: Three Continents Press, 1982.

Hall, A. Oakey. *The Manhattaner in New Orleans.* New York: 1851.

Hamlin, Talbot Faulkner. *Benjamin Henry Latrobe.* New York: Oxford University Press, 1955.

_____. *Greek Revival Architecture in America.* New York: Oxford University Press, 1944. Reprint. New York: Dover, 1975.

Harrap, Neil. *The Garden District.* New Orleans: 1969.

Hearn, Lafcadio. *Creole Sketches.* Boston: 1924.

Hermann, Bernard M. and Charles Dufour. *New Orleans.* Baton Rouge: Louisiana State University Press, 1980.

Herrin, M. H. *The Creole Aristocracy.* New York: Exposition Press, 1952.

Hewett, Mark Alan. *The Architect and the American Country House.* New Haven: Yale University Press, 1990.

Hosmer, Charles B., Jr. *Presence of the Past.* New York: G. P. Putnam's Sons, 1965.

Huber, Leonard V., compiler. *Landmarks of New Orleans.* New Orleans: Louisiana Landmarks Society and Orleans Parish Landmarks Commission, 1984.

_____. *Jackson Square Through the Years.* New Orleans: The Friends of the Cabildo, 1982.

Jackson, Joy J. *New Orleans in the Gilded Age.* Baton Rouge: Louisiana State University Press, 1969.

Janssen, James S. *Building New Orleans, The Engineer's Role.* New Orleans: Waldemar S. Nelson and Company, 1987.

Judr   h. "New Orleans and Her River." *National Geographic.* o. 2 (February 1971): 151–187.

K   n R. *New Orleans.* New Orleans: The Preservation   urce Center, 1981.

Ken   , John Smith. *History of New Orleans.* 3 vols. Chicago and New York: 1927.

Kennedy, Roger G. *Orders From France.* New York: Alfred A. Knopf, 1989.

Keyes, Frances Parkinson. *The Chess Players.* New York: Farrar, Straus and Cudahy, 1960.

King, Grace. "New Orleans, The Crescent City." In *Historic Towns of the Southern States,* Lyman P. Powell, ed. New York: 1900.

_____. *New Orleans: The Place and the People.* New York: 1895.

Kniffen, Fred B. *Louisiana: Its Land and People.* Baton Rouge: Louisiana State University Press, 1968.

Landry, Stuart O. *History of The Boston Club.* New Orleans: Pelican

Publishing Company, 1938.

Lane, Mills. *Architecture of the Old South: Louisiana.* New York: Abbeville Press, 1990.

Latrobe, Benjamin Henry Boneval. *Impressions Respecting New Orleans.* Edited with an introduction and notes by Samuel Wilson, Jr. New York: Columbia University Press, 1951.

Laughlin, Clarence John. *The Personal Eye.* Philadelphia: Aperture, Inc., 1973.

Lemann, Bernard. *The Vieux Carré —A General Statement.* New Orleans: Tulane University School of Architecture, 1966.

Lewis, Pierce F. *New Orleans, The Making of an Urban Landscape.* Cambridge, Mass.: Ballinger Publishing Company, 1976.

Logan, William Bryant and Vance Muse. *The Smithsonian Guide to Historic America: The Deep South.* New York: Stewart, Tabori & Chang, 1989.

McDermott, John Francis. *Frenchmen and French Ways in the Mississippi Valley.* Urbana, Ill.: University of Illinois Press, 1969.

McGee, Victor and Robert Brantley. *Greek Revival to Greek Tragedy, Henry Howard, Architect.* Unpublished manuscript, 1983.

Marcou, O'Leary & Associates, eds. "Plan and Program For the Preservation of the Vieux Carré." New Orleans: City of New Orleans, 1968.

Miller, Henry. *Letters to Anais Nin.* New York: Paragon House, 1988.

Morrison, Hugh. *Early American Architecture.* New York: Oxford University Press, 1952.

Norman's New Orleans and Environs. New Orleans: 1845.

Percy, Walker. *The Moviegoer.* New York: The Noonday Press, 1962.

Poesch, Jessie. *The Art of the Old South, 1560–1860.* New York: Alfred A. Knopf, 1983.

Pratt, Richard. *A Treasury of Early American Houses.* New York: McGraw Hill Book Company, 1949.

Ralph, Julian. "New Orleans, Our Southern Capital." *Harper's Magazine.* 86 (February 1893): 364–85.

Reinders, Robert C. *End of an Era, New Orleans, 1850–1860.* New Orleans: Pelican Publishing Company, 1964.

Ricciuti, Italo William. *New Orleans and Its Environs, 1727–1870.* New York: William Helburn, Inc., 1938.

Rice, Anne. *Interview with the Vampire.* New York, Ballantine Books, 1976.

Ripley, Alexandra. *New Orleans Legacy.* New York: Warner Books, 1988.

Roberts, W. Adolphe. *Lake Pontchartrain.* New York: The Bobbs-Merrill Company, 1938.

Rubin, Louis D., Jr. *George W. Cable . . . A Southern Heretic.* New York: Pegasus, 1969.

St. Martin, H. Paul III. "Colonial Images of New Orleans." New Orleans: Unpublished manuscript for Tulane University, 1991.

Samuel, Martha Ann Brett and Ray Samuel. *The Great Days of the Garden District.* New Orleans: Louise S. McGehee School, 1978.

Sanders, Isabel and Cindy Schoenberger. *The Historic Garden District.* New Orleans: Voulez-Vons, Inc., 1988.

Saxon, Lyle. *Fabulous New Orleans.* New York: D. Appleton-Century Company, 1928.

_____, ed. *Louisiana, A Guide to the State.* New York: Hastings House, 1941.

Saxon, Lyle and Robert Tallant. *Gumbo Ya Ya.* Boston: Houghton Mifflin Company, 1945.

Schuler, Stanley. *Mississippi Valley Architecture.* Exton, Pa.: Schiffer, 1984.

Scully, Arthur, Jr. *James Dakin, Architect.* Baton Rouge: Louisiana State University Press, 1973.

Smith, Joseph Frazer. *White Pillars.* New York: William Helburn, 1941.

Smith, G. E. Kidder. *The Architecture of the United States. 2: The South and Midwest.* Garden City, N. Y.: Anchor Books, 1981.

Somers, Dale A. *The Rise of Sports in New Orleans 1850–1900.* Baton Rouge: Louisiana State University Press, 1972.

Soniat, Meloncy C. "The Faubourgs Forming the Upper Section of the City of New Orleans." *Louisiana Historical Quarterly.* 20 (January 1937): 192–99.

Stadiem, William. *A Class by Themselves, "The Untold Story of the Great Southern Families."* New York: Crown Publishers, Inc., 1980.

Stanforth, Deirdre. *Romantic New Orleans.* New York: Penguin Books, 1977.

Starr, S. Frederick. *Southern Comfort, The Garden District of New Orleans, 1800–1900.* Cambridge, Mass.: The MIT Press, 1989.

Stevens, Patricia Land., ed. *Louisiana's Architectural and Archaeological Legacies.* Natchitoches, La.: Northwestern State University Press, 1982.

Street, James. "Louisiana." In *American Panorama, West of the Mississippi.* A Holiday Magazine Book. Garden City, N. Y.: Doubleday & Company, Inc., 1960.

Tishler, William H., ed. *American Landscape Architecture.* Washington, D.C.: The Preservation Press, 1989.

Tregle, Joseph G., Jr. "Early New Orleans Society: A Reappraisal." *Journal of Southern History.* 18 (February 1952): 20–36.

Twain, Mark. *Life on the Mississippi.* New York: Harper & Brothers, 1896.

Vlach, John Michael. "The Shotgun House: An African Architectural Legacy." In *Common Places, "Readings in American Vernacular Architecture."* Athens, Ga.: The University of Georgia Press, 1986.

Vogt, Lloyd. *New Orleans Houses, "A House-Watcher's Guide."* Gretna, La.: Pelican Publishing Company, 1985.

Ward, W. H. *The Architecture of The Renaissance in France, 1495–1830.* New York: Hacker Art Books, 1976. Second edition, Revised and Enlarged, London: 1926 of London: 1911.

Warner, Charles Dudley. "New Orleans." *Harpers New Monthly Magazine.* 74 (January 1887): 186–206.

Williams, Tennessee. *Memoirs.* Garden City, N. Y.: Doubleday & Co., Inc., 1975.

_____. *A Streetcar Named Desire.* New York: Signet, 1947.

Wilson, Charles Reagan and William Ferris, eds. *Encyclopedia of Southern Culture.* Chapel Hill: The University of North Carolina Press, 1989.

Wilson, Samuel, Jr. *Bienville's New Orleans, "A French Colonial Capital, 1716–1768."* New Orleans: The Friends of the Cabildo, 1968.

_____. *Collected Essays. "The Architecture of Colonial Louisiana."* Lafayette, La.: University of Southeastern Louisiana, 1987.

_____. "Evolution in a Historic Area's 'Tout Ensemble.'" In *Old and New Architecture, Design Relationship.* Washington, D.C.: The Preservation Press, 1980.

_____. *Plantation Houses on the Battlefield of New Orleans.* New Orleans: Louisiana Landmarks Society, 1965.

_____. "The Survey in Louisiana in the 1930s." In *Historic America, "Buildings, Structures, and Sites."* Washington, D.C.: Library of Congress, 1983.

_____. *Vieux Carré Historic District Demonstration Study.* New Orleans: City of New Orleans, 1968.

_____, ed. *Southern Travels, Journal of John H. B. Latrobe, 1834.* New Orleans: The Historic New Orleans Collection, 1986.

_____, foreword. *Over New Orleans.* Baton Rouge: Louisiana State University Press, 1983.

Zacharic, James S. *New Orleans Guide.* New Orleans: 1902.